KU-298-851

Individual Economic Decision-Making

Rational Economic Decision-Making

Utility refers to consumer satisfaction. Traditional economics assumes that:

- individuals want to maximise their utility, i.e. achieve the highest level of satisfaction possible
- businesses want to maximise their profits, i.e. achieve the highest level of profits possible.

Utility

Total utility is the total satisfaction received from consumption.

Marginal utility is the extra satisfaction gained from consuming an additional unit of the product. It shows how much total utility changes when another unit of a product is consumed.

The **Law of Diminishing Marginal Utility** states that additional units of consumption will eventually lead to falling marginal utility. For example, if you keep eating chocolate, at some point an extra chocolate bar will give you less extra satisfaction than the previous one.

Marginal and Total Utility

- If marginal utility is positive, total utility is increasing.
- If marginal utility is positive but falling, total utility is increasing but at a slower rate.
- If marginal utility is zero, total utility is maximised. It is not increased by consuming another unit.
- If marginal utility is negative (e.g. an extra chocolate bar made you feel worse, because you felt ill), total utility falls.

Paradox of Value

The difference between marginal and total utility is illustrated by the paradox of value.

There is a lot of water around in the UK and the population consumes high quantities of it. The total utility gained from water is very high, but the extra utility is low – this is why people are not prepared to pay very much for it, even though it is essential to life.

Diamonds by comparison are in short supply. The marginal utility of an extra diamond is very high

because there are so few of them. People are willing to pay much more for a diamond than water, even though they are not essential to life. The total utility of diamonds is low.

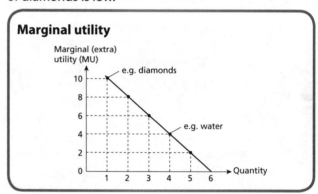

Marginal utility

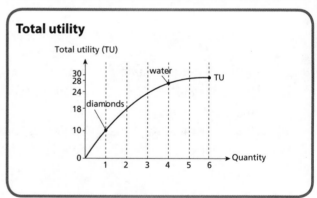

Total utility

Marginal Utility and Price

When considering whether to buy more of a product:

- a consumer will consider the marginal utility of a unit in relation to the price paid
- the consumer will compare this to the marginal utility of other products in relation to their price
- if the extra satisfaction per pound is higher than for other products, the consumer will consume more units
- this will continue, leading to lower marginal utility from the extra units of these products, until the marginal utility per pound is the same across all products.

This is known as the **equi-marginal condition** and it maximises utility.

NMURF

A-level
In a Week

Economics

AQA

Year 2

Andrew Gillespie

CONTENTS

Behavioural Economics

In traditional economic theory, it is assumed that consumers aim to maximise their utility. In reality, this may not be the case. **Behavioural economics** introduces psychology to traditional economics to try and understand decision-making more effectively.

Influences on Decision-Making

Although consumers often think of themselves as rational, there are many aspects of the decision-making process that are not. Some examples follow.

Bounded Rationality

In the 1950s, Herbert Simon highlighted that employees have **bounded rationality**, i.e. they:

- often have time constraints
- do not have perfect information
- have 'cognitive limitations'.

This means that people cannot solve problems optimally, but take shortcuts to enable decision-making to be easier and quicker. Consumers are the same. They do not take optimal decisions.

Individuals often rely on 'rules of thumb' to help cope with complex decisions. **Heuristics** are mental shortcuts used in decision-making that allow you to make quick decisions.

Bounded Self-Control

Traditional theory suggests that people have self-control and make rational decisions. However, it is more likely that people have **bounded (or limited) self-control**. For example, they may want to lose weight, drink less or stop smoking, but do not always have the self-control to do so. This is why people sometimes join schemes or organisations to help them change their behaviours.

Anchors

Anchors create a reference point and a bias in favour of a particular decision. For example, if a shop has a sign saying 'was £20, now £15', the first price is the anchor. The lower price seems more attractive in comparison to the anchor.

Status Quo Bias

Status quo bias refers to the fact that some individuals continue with a choice even after the decision has lost some or all of its benefit. For example, an individual might join a bank based on an initial offer and then stay for years, even when other banks are offering better incentives.

Status quo bias creates a form of inertia. It helps explain why producers can generate extra revenue by raising prices for long-standing customers.

Availability Bias

Availability bias suggests that individuals are influenced by the recent or significant events that are most easy to remember, i.e. those that are most available in the memory.

If the memory of an event is readily available:

- it is more likely to influence a decision than events that are difficult to remember
- individuals may overestimate its significance
- individuals may overestimate the likelihood that the event will occur again in future.

Social Norms

A **social norm** is a belief held by society or a group about how you should behave in a particular situation.

Individuals' decisions are influenced by people they want to be liked by and people they respect. They do not make decisions based solely on their own thoughts, but take into account what others would think.

This means that to change behaviour, governments should try to change society's view of what is and is not acceptable behaviour (e.g. in relation to drink-driving, smoking and drugs).

Altruism

Altruism is an unselfish concern for other people's welfare.

Standard economic theory assumes that people act out of self-interest rather than to help others. Behavioural theory recognises that people sometimes want to 'do the right thing' and have a sense of fairness and what is right. For example, employers might pay loyal staff above the market wage rate because they think it is fair and the right thing to do.

Behavioural Nudge

- A **nudge** is a low-cost and simple technique used to change an individual's behaviour without reducing the number of choices available.
- **Choice architecture** is a term that was developed by Richard Thaler and Cass Sunstien (2008). It refers to influencing the choices people make by designing different ways to present the choices to them.

● Choice architects and policymakers aim to change people's behaviour using a nudge rather than legislation. The UK government has the Behavioural Insights Team (BIT), which uses nudge theory to improve social outcomes.

● A **frame** is the way that a choice is described and presented to individuals.

Altering the information that people are given and changing the way in which questions are framed will affect the choices made.

Decision and Imperfect Information

Economic agents, such as households, firms and governments, are constantly making decisions. They all want to use their resources efficiently and to achieve their objectives (e.g. maximise utility and profit).

To make the optimal decisions, the decision-makers need information. Otherwise they have to rely on gut instinct, which is risky and unlikely to lead to optimal outcomes. However, information is not always available or perfect, which can lead to inefficient decisions.

One issue is **asymmetric information**. This occurs when one of the parties in a transaction has more information than the other – there is an imbalance of information. It is not symmetric.

Asymmetric information can distort markets. For example, when selling a second-hand car:

● the seller knows more about the history of the car than the buyer

● there is the potential for the seller to mislead the buyer

● the imbalance of information and fear of being misled causes buyers to assume the car has problems

● this drives the prices of second-hand cars down lower than they would be with perfect information.

Another issue is a lack of awareness of the external effects of production or consumption. For example, unless the government intervenes, when driving a car a consumer will consider the private costs but not the effect in terms of pollution or the impact of congestion on other road users. The differences between private and social costs and benefits can lead to under or overconsumption in the free market and an inefficient allocation of resources.

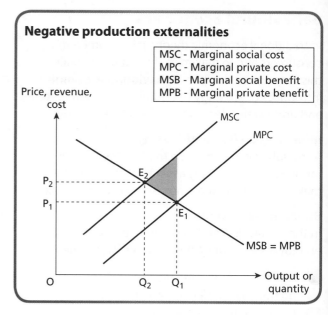

Negative production externalities

MSC – Marginal social cost
MPC – Marginal private cost
MSB – Marginal social benefit
MPB – Marginal private benefit

In this case, the social costs of production are greater than the private costs, e.g. due to pollution created during production. This means that inefficient decisions are made and the output in the market is higher than the socially optimal level.

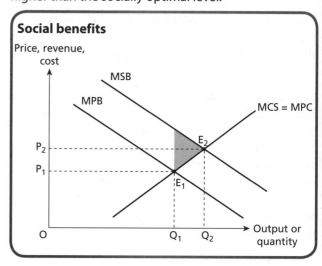

Social benefits

In this case, the social benefits of consumption are greater than the private benefits. For example, individuals might not appreciate the full benefits of healthcare and education. This can lead to inefficient decisions being made in the free market and under-consumption relative to the optimal level.

Behavioural Economics and Government Policy

The government often wants to change behaviour to achieve a more efficient allocation of resources. It may want people to consumer more (e.g. education or vaccinations) or less (e.g. smoking and drinking).

Traditional economic theory suggests that the government uses tools, such as taxes, to change the price.

Behavioural economics suggests the government might want to:

- frame choices in particular ways
- use social norms to influence behaviour
- create organisations to help people have more self-control.

SUMMARY

- **Traditional economic theory assumes consumers are rational and aim to maximise utility.**

- **The Law of Diminishing Marginal Utility means that the extra utility from consuming an additional unit will, at some point, fall.**

- **Behavioural economics recognises that consumers are not always rational.**

- **Various aspects of decision-making (e.g. anchoring, availability bias and bounded rationality) can lead to irrational choices.**

- **There are often information problems, such as asymmetric information or missing information, that lead to inefficient decisions regarding the allocation of resources.**

QUICK TEST

1. What is meant by 'marginal utility'?

2. What is meant by 'total utility'?

3. If marginal utility is positive but falling, what is happening to total utility?

4. What is meant by 'behavioural economics'?

5. What is meant by 'framing'?

6. What is meant by 'a nudge'?

7. What is meant by 'asymmetric information'?

8. What is meant by 'bounded rationality'?

9. A key difference between behavioural and traditional economic theory is that traditional theory assumes:

   A   consumers behave irrationally.

   B   consumers attempt to maximise profits.

   C   consumers consider a limited range of options when making a decision.

   D   consumers aim to maximise utility.

PRACTICE QUESTIONS

1. Using examples to illustrate your answer, explain why the buying behaviour of consumers might not be rational.   **[15 marks]**

2. The government would like to encourage people to drink less alcohol.
   Using your knowledge of both traditional economic theory and behavioural economics, assess alternative policies that the government might adopt to try to achieve this objective.   **[25 marks]**

3. a) Explain why, in a free market, consumers are likely to use their cars too much and the train too little.   **[15 marks]**

   b) Assess the extent to which the best way of reducing car usage is to increase the price of petrol.   **[25 marks]**

Returns to a Factor and Returns to Scale

The Short Run and the Long Run

In economics:

- the **short run** is the time period when at least one factor of production is fixed, e.g. a business may be committed to the rental of a building for a fixed period of time due to its contract
- the **long run** occurs when all factors of production are variable.

In the short run, production must be increased by adding variable factors of production to a fixed factor.

The fixed factor acts as a constraint. At some point, adding more variable factors to the fixed leads to a fall in the **marginal product** or **marginal returns** (change in output) from each additional unit of the variable factor. For example, if you keep adding labour to a fixed amount of physical space, at some point the workers will get in each other's way and the marginal product will fall.

Input-Output

- **Returns to a factor** occur in the short run as a variable factor is added to fixed factors.
- **Returns to scale** occur in the long run as the scale of production is changed with more of all factors.

Returns to a Factor and Costs

Both the returns to a factor and returns to scale show the relationship between inputs and output. They will both affect costs.

Productivity and Costs

Productivity and costs are usually inversely related, assuming all other factors remain constant, i.e. greater productivity leads to lower costs. This is because the business is getting more output from a given input.

If employees become less productive and are still paid the same wage, given that more of their time is used for each unit, the labour costs of these units are higher. If productivity increases then this means the output per worker is greater, and if wages are constant the labour cost per unit falls.

This is the reason why businesses focus so much on increasing productivity – it helps them achieve lower unit costs so they can be more price competitive.

The Law of Diminishing Returns

The **Law of Diminishing Returns** states that, in the short run, as successive units of a variable factor are added to a fixed factor of production, the marginal product (marginal returns) of the variable factor will eventually fall.

If the marginal product is positive but falling, the **total product** (or output) is still increasing but at a slower rate.

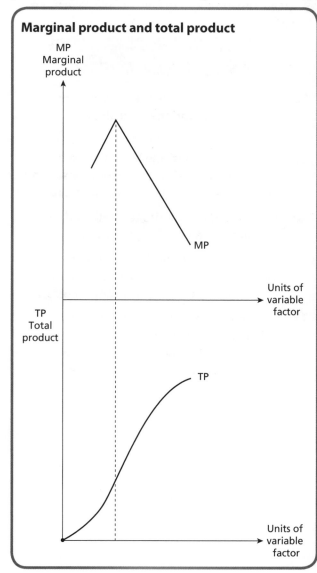

Marginal product and total product

Labour (units)	Total product (units)	Marginal product (units)
0	0	–
1	20	20
2	50	30
3	90	40
4	120	30
5	140	20
6	150	10

In the example above:

- there are increasing returns to a factor until the output of 90 units
- as the 4th, 5th and 6th employee is added, the marginal product falls, i.e. there are diminishing returns to a factor.

Average Product (Average Returns to a Factor)
Average product is the output per unit of the variable factor:

$$\text{Average product} = \frac{\text{total product}}{\text{number of variable factors}}$$

Example

200 units are produced by four employees.

$$\text{Average product (or output) per worker} = \frac{200}{4} = 50 \text{ units}$$

Marginal Product (Returns to a Factor) and Average Product (Returns to a Factor)
If the marginal product of the additional variable factor is above the average product, the average product will be pulled up, e.g. if a football team scored an average of two goals per match and then scored three or more in an extra match, it would pull the average up.

If the marginal product of the additional variable factor is below the average product, the average product will be pulled down, e.g. if a football team scored an average of two goals per match and then scored zero goals in an extra match, it would pull the average down.

This means the marginal product will cross the average product at the maximum of the average product.

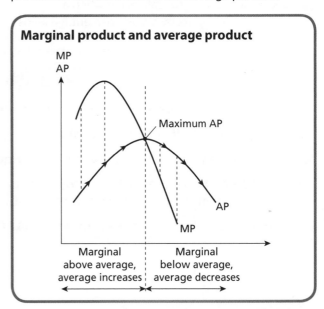

Marginal product and average product

Total product	Units of labour	Average product	Marginal product
100	1	100	–
300	2	150	200
600	3	200	300
760	4	190	160
880	5	176	120
900	6	150	20

Returns to Scale

Returns to scale occur when all inputs are increased. This occurs in the long run.

- Increasing returns to scale occur when an increase in all inputs by a given percentage leads to a more than proportionate increase in output. As a result, unit costs fall assuming no change in factor prices.
- Decreasing returns to scale occur when an increase in all inputs by a given percentage leads to a less than proportionate increase in output. As a result, unit costs rise assuming no change in factor prices.
- Constant returns to scale occur when an increase in all inputs by a given percentage leads to the same proportionate increase in output. As a result, unit costs rise assuming no change in factor prices.

SUMMARY

- **In the short run, one factor of production is fixed.**
- **In the long run, all factors are variable.**
- **Returns to a factor refer to the additional output from adding variable factors to a fixed factor.**
- **The Law of Diminishing Returns states that, at some point, additional units of a variable factor will lead to diminishing marginal returns (output).**
- **Returns to scale refer to the additional output from changing all the factors of production.**

1. The diagram below shows the short-run effect on output of increasing units of labour in combination with a fixed factor.

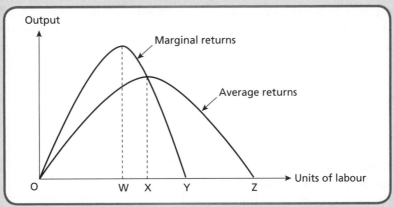

With reference to the diagram above:

a) At what level of output do diminishing marginal returns begin?

b) At what level of output is total output maximised?

c) Explain why marginal returns cross average returns at its maximum level.

2. Look at the table. At what point do diminishing returns start?

Number of employees	Total output
1	30
2	60
3	110
4	150
5	180
6	200

3. What is meant by the 'short run'?

4. If marginal product is falling but positive, what is happening to total product?

5. If marginal product is zero, what is happening to total product?

6. The average product of labour is 5 units and there are 12 employees. What is the total product?

7. a) If all inputs are doubled and output triples, there are increasing returns to scale. True or false?

    b) What will happen to average costs if all other factors are unchanged?

8. What is the difference between the short run and the long run in economics?

PRACTICE QUESTIONS

1. Explain why the Law of Diminishing Returns is likely to have an impact on a business's costs in the short run. **[6 marks]**

2. Explain why returns to scale are important determinants of unit costs in the long run. **[6 marks]**

Costs

- **Total cost** in the short run is made up of variable costs plus fixed costs.
- **Fixed costs** are costs that do not change with output, e.g. rent. They can change, but the change is not related to output levels.
- **Variable costs** are costs that do change with output, e.g. costs of raw materials.
- **Average cost** (sometimes called average total cost or unit cost) is the cost per unit:

$$\text{Average cost} = \frac{\text{total cost}}{\text{output}}$$

In the short run, the average cost (AC) is made up of the average variable cost (AVC) and the average fixed cost (AFC), i.e. the cost per unit is made up of the variable cost per unit and the fixed cost per unit.

AC = AFC + AVC

$$\frac{\text{total cost}}{\text{output}} = \frac{\text{fixed cost}}{\text{output}} + \frac{\text{variable cost}}{\text{output}}$$

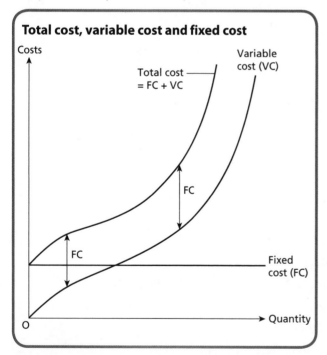

Total cost, variable cost and fixed cost

- Fixed costs are constant regardless of output.
- Variable costs are 0 when output is 0 (because there are no costs of production) and increase with more output.
- Total cost = fixed costs + variable costs

Average Fixed Cost (AFC)

The **average fixed cost (AFC)** will fall as output increases. This is because the fixed costs are spread over an increasing number of units.

Fixed costs (£)	Output (units)	Average Fixed Costs (£)
£1000	1	$\frac{£1000}{1} = £1000$
£1000	2	$\frac{£1000}{2} = £500$
£1000	3	$\frac{£1000}{3} = £333$
£1000	4	$\frac{£1000}{4} = £250$
£1000	5	$\frac{£1000}{5} = £200$

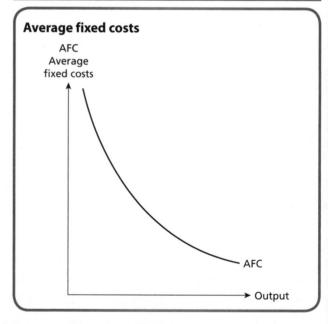

Average fixed costs

Average Variable Cost (AVC)

The shape of the **average variable cost (AVC)** curve is related to the average product curve.

An increase in average product means, on average, employees are producing more. Assuming all other factors are constant (including wage rates), the average cost per unit of labour falls and so the average variable cost falls.

A decrease in average product means, on average, employees are producing less. Assuming all other factors are constant (including wage rates), the average cost per unit of labour rises and so the average variable cost rises.

Average (Total) Cost, Average Variable Cost and Average Fixed Cost

The average total cost for any level of output equals average variable cost plus average fixed cost.

The average fixed costs fall as output increases, so the average total cost is increasingly determined by the average variable costs.

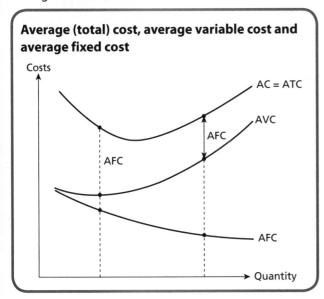

Average (total) cost, average variable cost and average fixed cost

Marginal Cost (MC)

Marginal cost (MC) is the extra cost of producing a unit:

$$\text{Marginal cost} = \frac{\text{change in total cost}}{\text{change in output}}$$

Output (units)	Total cost (£)	Marginal cost (£)
1	100	n/a
2	120	20
3	160	40
4	190	30
5	200	10
6	205	5

The shape of the marginal cost curve is the inverse (opposite) of the marginal product curve:

- If extra employees are becoming more productive, the extra cost of producing a unit will fall, all other factors unchanged (including wage rate).
- If extra employees are becoming less productive, the extra cost of producing a unit will rise, all other factors unchanged (including wage rate).
- If the marginal costs are positive and rising, the total costs are increasing at an increasing rate.
- If the marginal costs are positive and falling, the total costs are increasing at a decreasing rate.

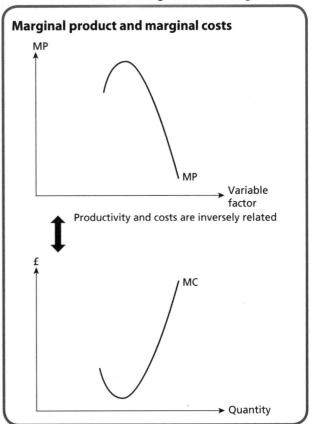

Marginal product and marginal costs

Productivity and costs are inversely related

Marginal Cost (MC) and Average Cost (AC)

- If the marginal cost is greater than the average cost, the average cost will increase, e.g. if the average cost per unit is £10 and the next unit costs £100 to make, it will pull up the average cost.
- If the marginal cost is less than the average cost, the average cost will decrease, e.g. if the average cost per unit is £10 and the next unit costs only £2 to make, it will pull down the average cost.

● This means the marginal cost will cross the average cost at its minimum point.

The relationship between marginal cost and average variable cost is the same:

● If the marginal cost is below the average variable cost, the average variable cost falls.
● If the marginal cost is above the average variable costs, the average variable cost rises.
● This means the marginal cost will cross the average variable cost at its minimum point.

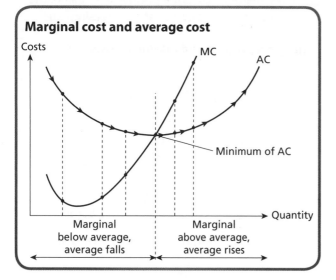

Marginal cost and average cost

Costs

MC

AC

Minimum of AC

Quantity

Marginal below average, average falls | Marginal above average, average rises

Long-Run Average Costs (LRAC)
The **long-run average cost (LRAC)** curve shows the minimum cost per unit with all factors variable.

At any moment a business is operating on a **short-run average cost (SRAC)** curve as there is a fixed factor of production.

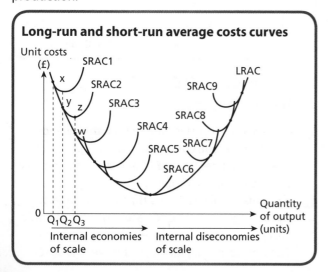

Long-run and short-run average costs curves

Unit costs (£)

SRAC1
x
SRAC2
y
z
SRAC3
w
SRAC4
SRAC5
SRAC6
SRAC7
SRAC8
SRAC9
LRAC

0
$Q_1 Q_2 Q_3$

Quantity of output (units)

Internal economies of scale | Internal diseconomies of scale

In the short run, a business can only increase output by adding variable factors to a fixed factor. This will lead to diminishing returns to a factor and the SRAC curve will be U-shaped.

A SRAC curve shows the minimum cost per unit for any level of output given a certain level of fixed factors, e.g. to increase output from Q_1 to Q_2 in the short run, the average costs might fall to x.

Over time, the business can change the level of a particular fixed factor to the optimal quantity. Unit costs now fall to y.

To increase output further in the short run, the business must expand with its given level of the fixed factor. If output increases to Q_3, the unit cost will be z.

However, over time the business can change to the optimal combination of factors and the average costs falls to w. It is now operating on a new SRAC curve.

At any moment in time, the business is on a SRAC curve reflecting the unit costs given a level of the fixed factor.

Over time, the business can move from one SRAC curve to another as it changes the factors of production. The LRAC curve is derived from all the SRAC curves.

- Total costs are made up of variable costs plus fixed costs in the short run.
- Fixed costs are costs that do not change with output.
- Variable costs are costs that do change with output.
- Average cost is the cost per unit. It is found by dividing total costs by output.
- Marginal cost is the extra cost of producing a unit.
- $\text{Marginal cost} = \dfrac{\text{change in total cost}}{\text{change in output}}$
- The long-run average cost (LRAC) curve shows the minimum cost per unit with all factors variable.
- A short-run average cost (SRAC) curve shows the minimum cost per unit for any level of output given a certain level of fixed factors.
- The minimum efficient scale (MES) is the first level of output at which the long-run average costs are minimised.

QUICK TEST

1. Explain what is meant by 'average fixed cost'.

2. Explain why the average variable cost and average total cost converge as output increases.

3. Unit costs are £40 and output is 25 units. What are total costs?

4. Average total cost is £30 and average variable cost is £25. Output is 40 units. What is the fixed cost?

5. Explain why average fixed costs fall with more output.

6. If marginal costs are positive and increasing, what is happening to total costs?

7. If marginal cost is 0, what is happening to total costs?

8. If total costs are £20 000 and fixed costs are £12 000 and output is 400 units, what is the average variable cost?

9. If total costs are £400 and average costs are £5 what is the output level?

10. Explain the relationship between the short-run and long-run average cost curves.

11. Explain the relationship between marginal and average costs.

PRACTICE QUESTION

1. Explain why the Law of Diminishing Returns is an important determinant of costs in the short run and internal economies of scale are important in the long run.   **[15 marks]**

Economies and Diseconomies of Scale

Internal economies of scale occur when the scale of production increases and causes the average cost to fall.

Purchasing Economies
If a business buys supplies and materials in bulk, it can buy more and get better deals, which reduce unit costs.

Technical Economies
The Law of Increased Dimensions
If storage or transport facilities are built on a larger scale, the amount that can be stored or transported increases faster than the costs of building the space.

For example, if a warehouse is a cube of side length 100 m:

- the footprint of the warehouse (space needed to build) is $(100 \times 100 =)$ 10 000 m^2
- the volume (total space inside warehouse) is $(100 \times 100 \times 100 =)$ 1 000 000 m^3

If the warehouse is built twice as big:

- the footprint is 40 000 m^2, i.e. 4 times bigger
- the volume is 8 000 000 m^3, i.e. 8 times bigger.

The firm would spend 4 times as much to hold 8 times as much, so the storage costs per unit fall.

Indivisibilities
Some capital equipment is **indivisible** and needs to be used on a large scale to be cost efficient. For example, if a small farm has a tractor, the tractor might be idle for much of the time and so its cost per unit of crop is high. As the farm grows, the tractor is used more fully and its cost per unit of crop falls.

Managerial Economies
As a business grows, the number of managers will not increase at the same rate, e.g. the number of employees might grow from one to ten, but there is still one manager. Therefore, management costs are spread over a greater number of units of output.

Financial Economies
As a business increases in size, it will have more assets. Therefore, it may be perceived as less of a risk to lenders, so they charge lower **interest rates** on loans.

Internal Diseconomies of Scale
Internal diseconomies of scale occur when the average cost falls as the scale of production increases.

Diseconomies of scale are linked to the problems of managing a larger business. For example:

- communication problems – there are more people to communicate with, possibly in different departments and locations
- control problems – it can be more complex and expensive to control more people
- coordination problems – it can be more complex and expensive coordinating more people.

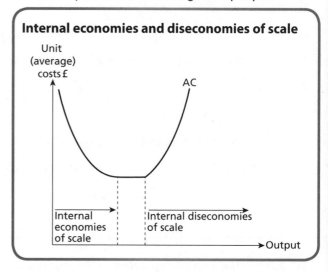

Internal economies and diseconomies of scale

The Shape of the Long-Run Average Cost Curve
- If internal economies and diseconomies of scale exist, the LRAC curve will be U-shaped.
- If internal diseconomies of scale do not exist, the LRAC curve may be L-shaped.

Minimum Efficient Scale (MES)

The **minimum efficient scale (MES)** is the first level of output at which the long-run average costs are minimised.

This is significant because, to gain a cost advantage, a business might want to expand up to the MES. However, there are no further unit cost gains from getting any bigger.

Minimum efficient scale

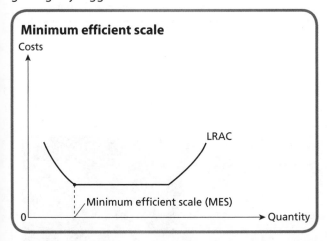

Industry Structure

The structure of an industry is likely to depend on how big the MES is relative to demand in the industry.

The higher the MES relative to demand, the fewer businesses you would expect to find in the industry. This is because a business would have to be operating at a relatively high scale to be efficient. This is especially true if the cost disadvantage of not being at MES is high – it will encourage firms to expand to the MES.

The lower the MES relative to demand, the more businesses you would expect to find in the industry. This is because there is no incentive to grow particularly big, so many businesses can operate efficiently. This is especially true if the cost disadvantage of not being below MES is low – there can be inefficient, smaller firms competing as well.

The MES is relatively high compared to demand

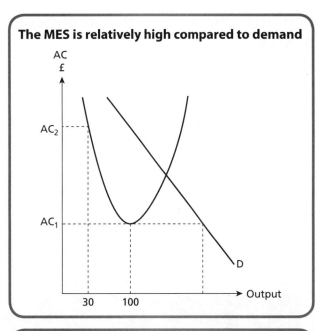

The MES is relatively small compared to demand

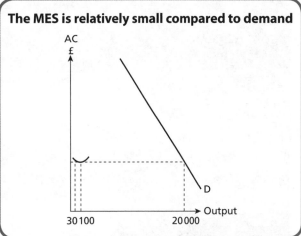

Minimum Efficient Scale as a Barrier to Entry

If the MES is high and if the average cost disadvantage of not being at the MES is significant, it will be difficult for other businesses to enter the industry.

There is a significant incentive to grow to a relatively large size to benefit from internal economies of scale, so entering on a smaller scale means the business is very inefficient and unlikely to be able to compete.

The cost structure of the industry is acting as a barrier to entry.

External Economies and Diseconomies of Scale

External economies of scale occur when the unit cost changes at each and every level of output. These changes occur due to factors outside the business.

For example, external economies and diseconomies of scale may be due to the location of the business:

- if the area has a good infrastructure and training courses are already available, the unit costs will decrease at every level of output
- if skilled labour in the area is expensive (perhaps because of a shortage), the unit costs will increase at every level of output.

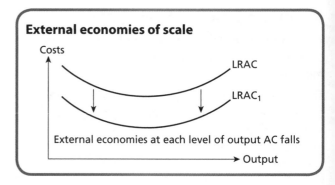

External economies of scale

Costs

LRAC

LRAC$_1$

External economies at each level of output AC falls

Output

If skilled labour in the area is expensive, unit costs will increase at every level of output.

SUMMARY

● Internal economies of scale occur when unit costs fall with an increase in the scale of production.

● External economies of scale occur when the unit costs fall at all levels of output due to factors outside of the business.

● The minimum efficient scale occurs at the first level of output at which long run average costs are minimised.

QUICK TEST

1. Explain **one** internal economy of scale.

2. Explain **one** internal diseconomy of scale.

3. What are 'external economies of scale'?

4. What is the 'minimum efficient scale'?

5. Economies of scale occur in the short run. True or false?

6. Economies of scale occur when costs fall as the scale of production increases. True or false?

7. External economies of scale occur when average costs fall as output increases. True or false?

8. In the long run all factors of production are variable. True or false?

PRACTICE QUESTIONS

1. To what extent is the structure of a market likely to be determined by the minimum efficient scale? [25 marks]

2. Discuss the view that the average costs of a business will inevitably increase as its scale of production increases. [25 marks]

Revenues and Profits

Total revenue (TR) measures the total spending (or total expenditure) by consumers.

Total revenue = price per unit × number of units sold

Average revenue (AR) measures the average price per unit.

$$\text{Average revenue} = \frac{\text{total revenue}}{\text{number of units sold}}$$

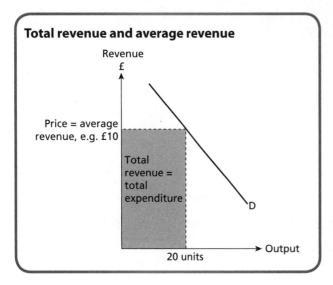

Total revenue and average revenue

In the diagram above:
- ● average revenue is the price of £10 a unit
- ● total revenue (total expenditure) = £10 × 20 units = £200

Marginal revenue (MR) measures the revenue earned by the sale of an extra unit.

$$\text{Marginal revenue} = \frac{\text{change in total revenue}}{\text{change in output}}$$

Marginal revenue shows the change in total revenue:
- ● If marginal revenue is positive, total revenue will increase.
- ● If marginal revenue is 0, total revenue will not increase – it is maximised.
- ● If marginal revenue is negative, total revenue will fall.

A Downward-Sloping Demand Curve and Marginal Revenue

If the demand curve is downward sloping, the price (average revenue) must be reduced to sell another unit.

For a single price monopolist, this reduction will be on the last unit and all the previous units as well. The greater the number of units being sold, the greater the number of units affected by the price reduction. This means the marginal revenue diverges from the demand curve.

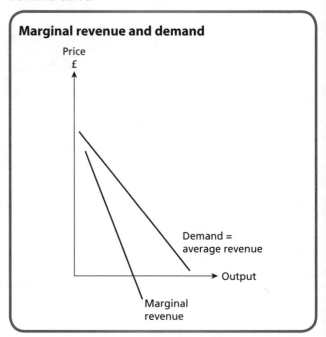

Marginal revenue and demand

If the marginal revenue falls but remains positive, the total revenue will still increase but at a slower rate.

Average revenue or price (£)	Units demanded	Total revenue (£)	Marginal revenue (£)
10	1	10	n/a
9	2	18	8
8	3	24	6
7	4	28	4
6	5	30	2

Price Elasticity of Demand and Total Revenue

When demand is **price inelastic**, the percentage change in quantity demanded is less than the percentage change in price, all other factors unchanged. The value of the price elasticity of demand (ignoring the sign) is less than 1.

In this situation, a price increase will increase revenue. The price per unit is higher and the fall in quantity demanded is smaller than the percentage increase in price.

When demand is **price elastic**, the percentage change in quantity demanded is greater than the percentage change in price, all other factors unchanged. The value of the price elasticity of demand (ignoring the sign) is greater than 1.

In this situation, a price increase decreases revenue. The price per unit is higher but the fall in quantity demanded is so great that overall revenue falls.

Price change	Price elasticity of demand	Effect on revenue
price increase	price inelastic demand	revenue increases
price decrease	price inelastic demand	revenue decreases
price increase	price elastic demand	revenue decreases
price decrease	price elastic demand	revenue increases

The Marginal Condition

It is usually assumed that a business wants to maximise its profit, i.e. achieve the biggest positive difference between total revenue and total costs.

To identify the profit-maximising output, the **marginal condition** can be used. This considers the extra (marginal) revenue from selling a unit and the marginal (extra) cost.

A business will **profit maximise** if it produces where marginal revenue equals marginal cost.

If marginal revenue is greater than marginal cost, a profit is made on the extra unit and total profits will increase if another unit is sold. The business should produce all units up to the point where marginal revenue and marginal cost are equal and there are no further profits to be made.

If marginal revenue is less than marginal costs, a loss will be made if this unit is produced and sold. This

will reduce total profits. A profit-maximising business should not produce these units.

Relationship of marginal revenue and marginal costs	Impact on required output level to profit maximise
marginal revenue > marginal cost	• produce another unit • there is extra profit to be made
marginal revenue = marginal cost	• profit maximising • no extra profit to be made
marginal revenue < marginal cost	• do not produce the unit • this unit would make a loss

Normal Profits

In economics, costs are assumed to include the opportunity cost of resources. This means that if the revenue earned covers the costs, the business is earning just enough to keep resources in their present use.

In accounting terms, the business is actually earning a profit when total revenue equals total costs (because accountants do not include opportunity costs when calculating the costs of the business). This provides the level of returns required to justify using resources in this way. When revenue equals total costs, a business is said to be earning **normal profit**.

Abnormal Profits

If the total revenue is greater than the total costs, the business is earning rewards higher than those needed to keep resources in their present use. This is called **abnormal**, **supernormal** or **supranormal profit**.

The abnormal profits are an incentive for businesses in other industries to try and enter the industry.

Losses

If total revenue is less than total costs, the business is making a **loss**. The rewards being earned are less than the rewards required to keep resources in their present use. Businesses will want to leave the industry because the rewards are not high enough to justify being there.

Contribution

If the revenue is greater than the variable costs, a **contribution** is made towards fixed costs. For example, if revenue is £200 and variable costs are £160, there is a £40 contribution towards the fixed costs.

Contribution = revenue − variable costs

Contribution per unit = price per unit − variable costs per unit

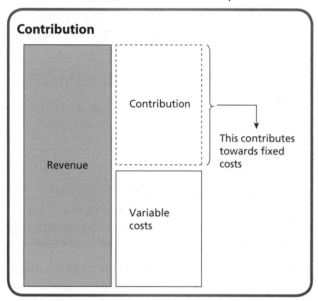

Break-Even Point

In the long run, a business will not keep producing if it is making a loss – it will shut down.

In the long run, a business will only produce if the price at least equals the average cost (i.e. total revenue equals total costs). When the price just equals the average cost, this is known as the **break-even point**.

Shutdown Point

In the short run, a business must pay fixed costs (such as rent) even if there is no output. If it does not produce, it will lose an amount equal to fixed costs.

In the short run, the additional costs of producing (as opposed to not producing) are the variable costs. If the revenue earned at least covers the variable costs, it is worth producing. If it more than covers the variable costs, a contribution is being made towards paying off the fixed costs.

In the short run, therefore, a business will produce provided the price at least covers the average variable cost (i.e. the revenue at least covers the variable costs). When the price just equals the average variable cost, this is known as the **shutdown point.**

Concept	Expressed per unit	Expressed in totals
normal profit	average revenue = average costs	total revenue = total costs
abnormal profit (supernormal profit)	average revenue > average costs	total revenue > total costs
loss	average revenue < average costs	total revenue < total costs
break-even point	average revenue = average costs	total revenue = total costs
shutdown point	average revenue = average variable costs	total revenue = variable costs

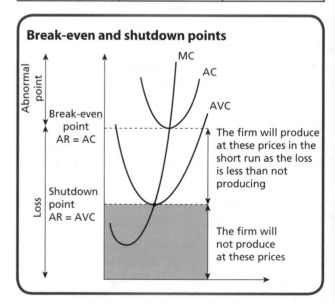

Break-even and shutdown points

- Marginal revenue is the revenue from selling an extra unit.
- Total revenue is the total spending by consumers on a business's products.
- Normal profit occurs if revenue equals costs.
- Abnormal profit occurs if revenue is greater than costs.
- Losses occur if revenue is less than costs.
- In the short run, a business will produce provided the price is greater or equal to the average variable cost. This is the shutdown point.
- In the long run, a business will produce provided the price is greater or equal to the average costs. This is the break-even point.

QUICK TEST

1. Look at the table.

Price (£)	Quantity demanded (units)
10	1
9	2
8	3
7	4
6	5

Which of the following is **true**?

A   average revenue is constant

B   total revenue is constant

C   marginal revenue falls

D   total revenue falls

2. A business produces 20 units of output per week. Its costs are as follows:

- marginal costs = £60
- average variable cost = £40
- average total cost = £50

What are the total fixed costs of the business?

A £1000   B £2000   C £200   D £10

3. Average fixed costs:

A   do not change with output.

B   increase with the Law of Diminishing Returns.

C   fall with output.

D   include the cost of raw materials.

4. At what point does the marginal cost curve cross the average cost curve and why?

5. What is meant by 'normal profit'?

6. Explain why the average variable cost curve and the average total cost curve get closer to each other as output increases.

7. Complete the following table.

Price change	Price elasticity of demand	Effect on revenue
price increase	price inelastic demand	
	price elastic demand	revenue decreases

PRACTICE QUESTIONS

1. Explain the relationship between marginal, average and total revenue. **[15 marks]**

2. Assess whether a loss-making business should carry on producing. **[25 marks]**

Perfect Competition

Market Structure

Market structure describes the number and size of the producers in the market.

There are several different market structures that can exist. They differ in terms of:

- how many businesses there are in the industry
- how big the businesses are
- how differentiated the products are
- how easy it is for businesses to enter or exit the industry.

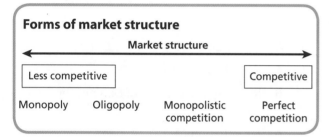

Forms of market structure

Market structure

← Less competitive ... Competitive →

| Monopoly | Oligopoly | Monopolistic competition | Perfect competition |

Perfect Competition

Perfect competition occurs when:

- there are many firms in the industry (large number of producers)
- products are identical (not differentiated)
- there is freedom of movement in and out of the industry in the long run
- customers have perfect knowledge of what products are available.

Each business in perfect competition is a **price taker**.

Each business is so small relative to the size of the industry that its output decisions (increasing or decreasing output) have no noticeable effect on the industry supply and do not change the market price. This means a business in perfect competition can sell all of its output at the same price. It faces a perfectly elastic demand curve.

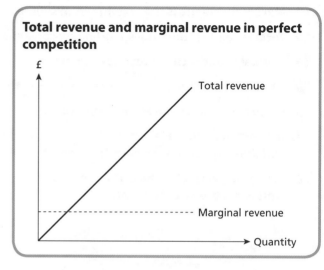

Total revenue and marginal revenue in perfect competition

Every unit is sold at the same price, so marginal revenue is constant, e.g. if every unit is sold at £10, the marginal revenue is £10 and the total revenue increases by £10.

The Short Run in Perfect Competition

In the short run, businesses can make abnormal profits, i.e. total revenue can be greater than total costs (price is greater than the average cost).

Abnormal profits act as a signal to other businesses to enter the industry because of the high returns being generated.

If several other businesses enter the industry, output will increase noticeably and shift the industry supply curve outwards. As the supply curve shifts outwards, this brings the market price down.

This process will continue until only normal profits are earned. At this point there is no further incentive to enter the industry, because the revenue being earned only just covers the costs (including the opportunity cost) of competing.

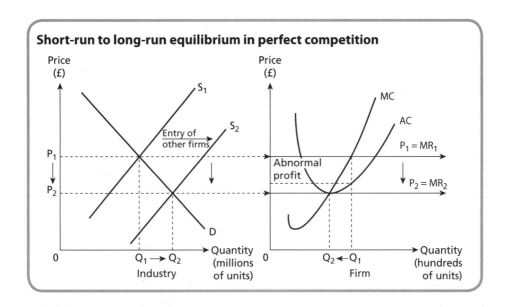

Short-run to long-run equilibrium in perfect competition

- The firm is assumed to be a profit-maximiser – it produces where marginal revenue equals marginal cost, so there is no extra profit to be made.
- In the short run, at output Q_1 and price P_1, the firm is making abnormal profit. This is because the price is greater than the average cost.
- This brings others into the industry, driving the price down to P_3.
- Firms profit maximise at P_2Q_2 making normal profits. There is no further incentive for firms to enter or leave the industry.

- In the short run, firms in perfect competition can make losses, e.g. at P_1Q_1. At this point, the revenue does not cover the total costs (the price is less than the average costs). This leads to exit by some businesses.
- As several businesses exit, the total output is reduced and the industry supply shifts inwards.
- The fall in supply will increase the industry price to P_2 until only normal profits are earned.
- Firms will produce at P_2Q_2. At this point there is no further incentive to leave the industry as the revenue is covering the costs (including the opportunity costs) of competing in this industry.

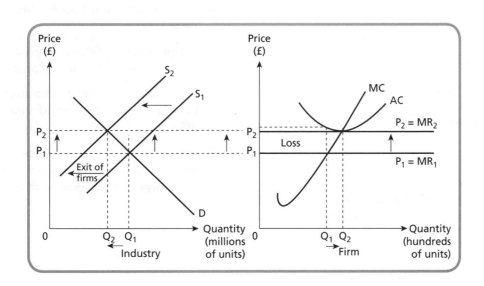

Long-Run Equilibrium in Perfect Competition

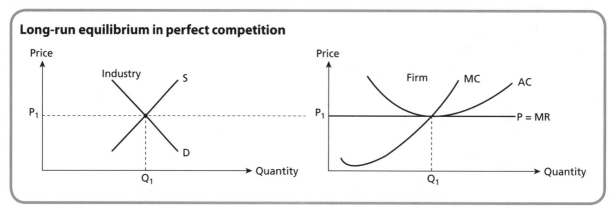

Long-run equilibrium in perfect competition

In the long run, in perfect competition businesses make **normal profits**. This is due to entry and exit and the lack of barriers to movement by businesses. Resources can move in and out of the industry over time.

There is **allocative efficiency**. This is because the price (which represents the extra benefit of a unit to the consumers) at which businesses sell equals the marginal cost of production. Assuming these costs and benefits represent the social marginal benefit and social marginal cost, producing where they are equal means that society's welfare (see page 28) is maximised.

There is **productive efficiency**. This is because firms produce at the minimum of the average cost curve – at the lowest unit cost possible

Is Perfect Competition Real?

A perfectly competitive market may not actually exist.

The market for some agricultural products may be the closest that exists to perfect competition. However, the model shows in theory (assuming no market failures) the conditions for efficient allocation of resources.

Other market structures can be compared to perfect competition in terms of efficiency. Therefore, this market structure provides a useful 'yardstick' for comparison.

Assumptions of Perfect Competition

A perfectly competitive market can lead to an efficient allocation of resources. This assumes there are no

market failures and the costs and benefits reflect the full social costs and benefits. It is known as a 'first-best world'.

In reality, there are many failures and imperfections – we live in a 'second-best world'. In this situation, a perfectly competitive market may not be socially optimal, for example, if it fails to take account of external costs and benefits.

SUMMARY

- A perfectly competitive market has many businesses, identical products, perfect information and freedom of entry and exit.

- In perfect competition, businesses are price takers.

- In the long run, firms in perfect competition make normal profits.

- In the long run, in perfect competition, firms are productively and allocatively efficient.

- Perfect competition provides a yardstick with which to compare the efficiency outcomes in other market structures.

1. State **two** assumptions of a perfectly competitive market.

2. What is meant by a firm being a 'price taker'?

3. What is meant by 'abnormal profits'?

4. In the long run, firms in perfect competition earn normal profits. True or false?

5. In the long run, firms in perfect competition are allocatively inefficient. True or false?

6. In perfect competition there is freedom of entry and exit. True or false?

7. Which of the following statements about firms in perfectly competitive industry is true?

   A   They are price makers.

   B   They sell all units at the same price.

   C   The price they sell at equals the average fixed cost.

   D   The price they sell at equals the total cost.

8. Allocative efficiency occurs where the price equals the average cost. True or false?

9. Productive efficiency occurs when output is at the level where average costs are minimised. True or false?

10. In perfect competition, the demand curve for a business is a horizontal line. True or false?

PRACTICE QUESTIONS

1. Explain why businesses in perfect competition can earn abnormal profits in the short run but make normal profits in the long run.   **[15 marks]**

2. To what extent is perfect competition the 'ideal' market structure?   **[25 marks]**

Monopoly and Monopsony

Monopoly

In a **monopoly**:

- there is a single seller
- there is no freedom of entry in the long run – there are barriers to entry
- the monopolist is a **price maker**, i.e. it sets the price in the market.

In a monopoly, the business can make abnormal profits even in the long run. Although other businesses may want to enter the market to benefit from the high rewards and compete away these profits, barriers to entry stop them from doing so.

A **pure monopoly** occurs when there is a single seller in a market. **Monopoly power** occurs when one business dominates the industry and has power over others. In the UK, for example, if a business has a **market share** of more than 25%, it is regarded as a monopoly.

A **statutory monopoly** occurs when a monopoly is created by the government and is protected by law. For example, a government may have only one provider of postal or train services.

Monopoly power can arise due to barriers to entry (factors that make it difficult for other firms to enter the industry), such as:

- legal protection, e.g. a government may allow only one provider of rail services or electricity, or it may be that a product's technology has legal protection (a patent), so others cannot copy the technology for a certain number of years
- high investment in marketing costs, e.g. advertising, making it difficult for other firms to enter and compete
- a highly differentiated product or high level of brand loyalty, making it difficult for new market entrants to win sufficient demand to survive
- a high **minimum efficient scale (MES)**, making it difficult to enter the market and compete due to higher unit costs – the existing business can cut the price and still make profit, but the entrant would make losses due to higher unit costs.

Barriers to entry can change over time. For example:

- a government may increase or reduce the barriers to entry into the domestic market for foreign goods
- technological development may reduce some barriers, e.g. businesses entering the travel agency market no longer need to invest in high street branches (a major investment) – they can simply operate online.

Monopoly and Demand

A monopolist faces a downward-sloping demand curve.

To sell more, the price has to be reduced on the last unit and on all the previous ones. This means:

- the marginal revenue lies below the demand curve
- the marginal revenue diverges from the demand curve because the greater the number of units sold, the greater the number of units affected when the price is cut.

Marginal revenue = price of last unit – reductions in the price on earlier units

A profit-maximising monopolist produces where marginal revenue equals marginal cost. This means there is no extra profit to be made.

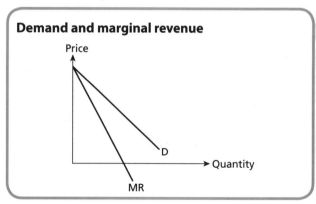

Demand and marginal revenue

A monopolist uses its power to:

- increase the **producer surplus** (the difference between the price producers are paid for a unit and the price they are willing to supply it at)
- reduce the **consumer surplus** (the difference between the price consumers pay for a unit and the price they are willing to pay for it).

Overall there is a welfare loss to society. The welfare of society is called **community surplus**.

Community surplus = producer surplus + consumer surplus

In order to increase its own profits, the monopolist restricts output and drives up price – some units are not produced and sold even though the price is greater than the extra cost.

- In a perfectly competitive industry, the equilibrium price and output would be P_0Q_0.
- A monopoly with the same demand and cost conditions will increase the price and decrease the quantity – this increases producer surplus, reduces consumer surplus and creates a welfare loss (it creates a deadweight social burden triangle).

- The monopolist produces at P_1Q_1.
- In a perfectly competitive industry with the same cost and demand conditions, the market price would be P_0 and market equilibrium output would be Q_0.
- Compared to perfect competition, the price is higher and the quantity lower in a monopoly.
- On units Q_1Q_0 the extra benefit to society (as shown by the price consumers are willing to pay) is greater than the extra costs (marginal costs). This means society would benefit from extra welfare if these units were produced.
- The shaded area represents a welfare loss to society – on these units the extra benefit is greater than the extra costs, so they should be produced. However, the monopolist does not want to produce them because it involves lowering the price on units Q_1Q_2 and on earlier units and this reduces its profit.

This is shown in more detail below.

The impact of monopoly on a perfectly competitive industry

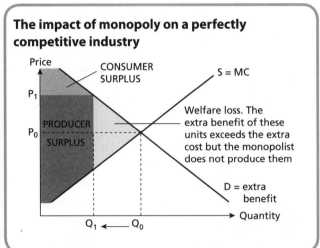

Monopoly and efficiency

Between Q_0 and Q_1 the extra benefit of the unit (shown by the price) exceeds the extra cost. Therefore welfare would increase if these were produced. This area is a welfare loss because Q_0Q_1 are not produced by a monopolist. It is allocatively inefficient.

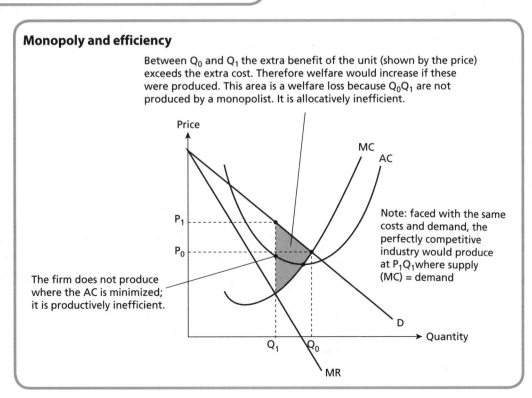

The firm does not produce where the AC is minimized; it is productively inefficient.

Note: faced with the same costs and demand, the perfectly competitive industry would produce at P_1Q_1 where supply (MC) = demand

Natural Monopoly

A **natural monopoly** occurs when the economies of scale are so great that:

- the MES is more than 100% of the market
- the cost disadvantages of not being at the MES are very high.

There is a great incentive for a business to expand to benefit from the cost savings and it is difficult for other firms to compete because of the cost disadvantages they would face. As a result, one business is likely to dominate – it is naturally a monopoly.

This occurs because of the major internal economies of scale within the industry. For example, in the communications industry there are significant indivisibilities. To produce a phone service, a provider must have a network – this has huge initial costs, but they can be spread over more and more users as the business attracts new customers. In such industries, high volumes are important to benefit from the internal economies of scale.

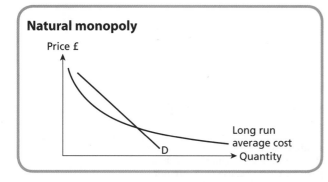

Natural monopoly

Monopoly and Efficiency

A monopolist is:

- **allocatively inefficient** because the price (marginal benefit) is greater than the marginal cost – society would benefit from additional units being prepared
- **productively inefficient** if the business is not producing at the minimum of the average cost curve – the cost per unit is higher than it could be
- **x-inefficient** (see page 46) – the barriers to entry mean there is a lack of incentive to keep costs down and a lack of competition means that management may become inefficient and motivation may fall, so costs may be higher than they would be in a more competitive market.

Potential Benefits of Monopoly Power

- The abnormal profits may act as an incentive to other businesses to innovate to try and destroy the existing monopoly and gain the abnormal profits. This process was named **creative destruction** by Joseph Schumpeter.
- Monopolies may restrict output relative to a more competitive market. If a negative production externality exists in an industry, restricting output may actually take the market nearer to the socially optimal level. Given that negative externalities are a market failure, monopolies may actually remedy this, leading to a more efficient allocation of resources.
- The abnormal profits may be used for research and development, which can lead to innovations and new technology that reduce costs over time. A monopoly may actually encourage innovation by other firms – this is known as **dynamic efficiency**.

Monopsony

A **monopsony** occurs when there is a single buyer of goods, services or labour in a market.

Monopsony power exists when the buyer has significant influence over the suppliers. For example:

- the government may be a single buyer of certain weapons in the defence sector
- the National Health Service may be the major buyer of doctors in the labour market
- the large supermarkets have major power over food suppliers and farmers
- airlines have major power over aircraft engine producers
- Amazon has major power over book publishers.

Average and Marginal Costs in a Monopsony

A monopsonist may face an upward-sloping supply curve.

Example

Number of workers	Wage rate = average cost (£)	Total wage costs (£)	Marginal costs of employing an extra worker (£)
10	20	200	n/a
11	22	242	42
12	25	300	58
13	30	390	90
14	35	490	100

The table illustrates some average cost of inputs. For example, in the labour market:

- if 10 workers will work for a wage rate of £20 an hour, this is the average cost of labour
- if 11 workers will work for a wage rate of £22, the average cost is £22.

However, the marginal cost takes account of the fact that to acquire another unit of labour, the wage must increase for that unit of labour and for all previous units, e.g. to attract the 11th worker, the wage rate must increase not just for the 11th worker but all the workers before them.

The marginal costs of the inputs will be above the supply curve and diverging.

Profit-Maximising Monopsonist in the Labour Market

The demand curve for a factor, such as labour, reflects the extra value of its output. This is called the **marginal revenue product** – it is the value of the extra output of the extra unit of labour.

A profit-maximising monopsonist will employ people up to the point where the marginal revenue product of labour is equal to the marginal cost of labour.

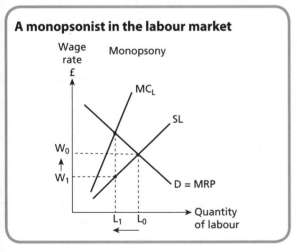

A monopsonist in the labour market

- L_1 employees will be employed at a wage rate of W_1.
- In the free market, equilibrium is at $W_0 L_0$.

A monopsonist employs fewer employees at a lower wage than would be the case in a free market.

Benefits of a Monopsony

- A monopsonist can use its bargaining power with suppliers to reduce its costs. This might lead to lower prices for consumers and / or increase profit. The profit may be distributed to owners or invested in research and development.

- The monopsony power may offset the monopoly power of suppliers. For example, the airlines have a great deal of power negotiating with the aircraft engine producers but, as there are relatively few of them, the producers are very powerful themselves. The major cinema chains have monopsony power but the major film studios have monopoly power.

QUICK TEST

1. What is meant by a 'monopoly'?
2. State **two** possible barriers to market entry.
3. If the price is greater than average costs, abnormal profits are made. True or false?
4. A monopoly is likely to have higher prices and higher output than a competitive industry. True or false?
5. Consumer surplus is likely to be higher in a monopoly than in a competitive industry. True or false?
6. What is meant by 'producer surplus'?
7. A monopolist is productively inefficient. True or false?
8. A monopolist may be dynamically efficient. True or false?

PRACTICE QUESTIONS

1. Explain why a monopolist is able to make abnormal profits in the long run. **[15 marks]**

2. **a)** Explain, with examples, why some markets are more difficult to enter than others. **[10 marks]**

   b) Discuss the extent to which monopoly markets should be encouraged by governments. **[15 marks]**

Other Market Structures

Oligopoly

An **oligopoly** exists when a few firms dominate an industry. For example, there are some large firms in the supermarket, banking and petrol industries that have a high market share (their sales are a high percentage of the total sales in the industry).

The market share of the top *n* firms is called the *n* **firm concentration ratio**. The higher the concentration ratio, the more dominant the firms are.

Example

Largest five firms in market	Market share (%)
A	25
B	22
C	20
D	18
E	12
Five firm concentration ratio	**97**

n firm concentration ratio (%)
$$= \frac{\text{sales of the largest } n \text{ firms in the industry}}{\text{total sales of the industry}} \times 100$$

Collusion and Competition

If firms decide to work together, this is known as **collusive behaviour**. For example, firms may decide to act together and set the price and output in the market.

Collusion may be:

- overt, i.e. the firms formally agree amongst themselves what they are going to do
- tacit (implied), e.g. firms decide not to have a price war – there is not a formal agreement, but they have an implicit understanding.

If firms decide to compete against each other, this is competitive or non-collusive behaviour.

Interdependence

Oligopolistic firms are **interdependent** – they consider the actions and reactions of other firms before deciding what to do. For example, they realise that if they cut price, other firms may decide to follow.

Competition

If firms are non-collusive they might compete in different ways.

Price Competition
Price Wars
Price wars occur when firms try to undercut each other to remove the competition. Once the competition leaves the industry due to losses, the remaining firms can increase prices again.

Limit Pricing
Limit pricing is where firms work out the highest price they can charge without encouraging entry to the market. The price is set so that if a firm enters, it will increase output and bring the market price down to the extent that losses would be made. This reduces the incentive to enter.

Rather than profit maximise and encouraging entry, existing firms accept a lower price and lower profits to deter entry. With limit pricing, fewer profits are made in any time period but greater profits could be earned in the long run as other firms do not enter the market.

Non-Price Competition
Non-price competition is about the way firms differentiate themselves from each other. For example, they may try to develop their brand positioning through advertising and promotions.

Game Theory

The firms in an oligopoly are interdependent. There are relatively few large firms and they will take account of the possible actions of others when deciding what to do. This is known as **game theory**.

Example
Firms A and B must decide whether to charge a high or low price in a market.

The diagram shows a payoff matrix.

		Firm B		
		High price		Low price
Firm A	High price	£100	£100	−£50 £90
	Low price	£90	−£50	£0 £0

- The top-left value in each box shows the payoff for Firm A.
- The bottom-right value shows the payoff for Firm B.
- If both firms cooperate and have a high price, they will maximise their profits.
- If Firm A lowers its price and Firm B does not, there will be gains for Firm A and losses for Firm B.
- If Firm B lowers its price and Firm A does not, there will be gains for Firm B and losses for Firm A.
- If they do not trust each other to keep to a high price and believe the other firm will charge a low price, they will both opt for a low price – this results in a £0 return for both firms. This payoff matrix shows that the optimal decision in this case would be for both firms to charge a high price, but because they may not trust each other, they may both choose a low price and end up worse off than they could be.

The Kinked Demand Curve Model

The **kinked demand curve model** is a non-collusive model – it assumes firms compete against each other.

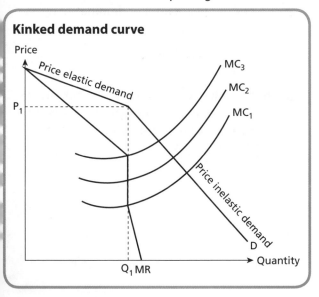

Kinked demand curve

Here are the assumptions of the kinked demand curve model if a firm has set a price of P_1:

- If the firm increases its price, this increase will not be followed by other firms in the industry. As a result, the demand curve is price elastic, i.e. demand is relatively sensitive to price. A price increase would lead to a more than proportionate decrease in quantity demanded and a fall in revenue. Therefore, there is no incentive to increase price.
- If the firm decreases its price, this decrease will be followed by other firms in the industry. As a result, the demand curve is price inelastic, i.e. demand is relatively insensitive to price. A price decrease would lead to a less than proportionate increase in quantity demanded and a fall in revenue. Therefore, there is no incentive to decrease price.

Assumptions of Perfect Competition

Price change	Behaviour of competitors	Effect on revenue
price increase	• others do not follow • demand is price elastic	revenue falls
price decrease	• others do follow • demand is price inelastic	revenue falls

Given the price elasticities of demand, revenue will fall if the price is increased or decreased, so there is no incentive for the firm to change price.

This model helps explain why:

- prices are relatively 'sticky' (do not change much) in oligopolies
- the focus in oligopoly is often on non-price competition.

Referring to the kinked demand curve diagram, there could be a change in the marginal costs between MC_1 and MC_3 and the profit-maximising output would still lead to P_1Q_1 (whereas in other markets, a change in costs would lead to a change in the profit-maximising price and output). This again explains why prices may be 'sticky'.

Cartels

In a **cartel**, a group of firms join together to act like a monopolist. This is a collusive oligopoly.

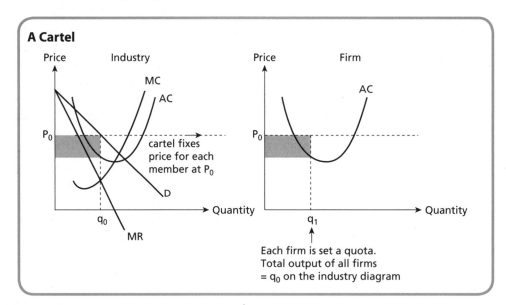

A Cartel

cartel fixes price for each member at P_0

Each firm is set a quota. Total output of all firms = q_0 on the industry diagram

A cartel can maximise the profits of the group as a whole. The price is set where the marginal revenue equals the marginal costs of the group. Each firm adopts the set price and the overall output is divided between the members of the group, i.e. each firm has a quota.

However, there is an incentive to cheat in a cartel – a member might sell more than their quota at the set price. This will increase the total output in the industry and drive down the price in the market.

Although the firm that cheats may increase its own profits, the profits for the industry as a whole will fall. This means cartels are unstable – individual firms may pursue their own interests at the expense of the group as a whole.

For cartels to work, they need to be effectively monitored to ensure no one is cheating. This can be difficult (e.g. trying to track all sales of oil around the world) and expensive.

SUMMARY

- An oligopoly is a market dominated by a few large firms.

- In an oligopoly, firms may compete or collude.

- In the kinked demand curve model, there is no incentive to change price as revenue is expected to fall – this is why prices are 'sticky'.

1. What is meant by 'collusion' in oligopoly?

2. Explain why prices may be 'sticky' in the kinked demand curve model.

3. What is meant by 'limit pricing'?

4. State **two** forms of non-price competition.

5. When price discriminating, the price is lower in a price inelastic market. True or false?

6. The prices charged by different petrol stations in any area of the UK tend to be similar. This is because:

   A the government sets the price.

   B firms believe that a price cut would be followed by others, but a price increase would not.

   C firms believe that a price cut would not be followed by others, but a price increase would.

   D the market is a monopoly.

7. The table describes the cost and revenue for two firms in long-run equilibrium.

Firm A	Firm B
AR > MR	AR > MR
AC = AR	AR > AC
AC > MC	AC > MC

   Identify the market structure that each firm operates within.

8. The kinked demand curve model assumes a lack of cooperation between firms. True or false?

9. A cartel assumes cooperation between firms. True or false?

10. An oligopoly market has many similar size firms in it. True or false?

11. Game theory assumes firms are independent of each other. True or false?

PRACTICE QUESTIONS

1. Discuss the view that oligopoly will lead to the same price and output in the market as a monpoly. **[25 marks]**

2. Discuss the view that non-price competition is more important than price as a means of competing with others in an oligopoly. **[25 marks]**

Monopolistic Competition and Price Discrimination

Monopolistic Competition

Monopolistic competition occurs when:

- there are many firms in an industry
- each firm is differentiated in some way, e.g. their products are differentiated
- there is freedom of entry and exit in the long run.

In the short run, a firm in monopolistic competition can make abnormal profits or losses. In the long run, a firm in monopolistic competition can only make normal profits.

The Short Run

In monopolistic competition, if abnormal profits are being earned in the short run:

- more firms will enter the market attracted by the high returns
- the demand curve for one firm will shift inwards until only normal profits are earned
- at this point, there is no further incentive to move.

If losses are being earned in the short run:
- firms will leave the market given the low returns being earned

- the demand curve for one firm will shift outwards until only normal profits are earned
- at this point, there is no further incentive to move.

The Long Run

In monopolistic competition, in the long run:

- only normal profits are earned, i.e. the price equals the average cost
- there is allocative inefficiency because the price paid (the extra benefit of the unit) is greater than the marginal (extra) cost
- assuming the benefits and cost represent the extra benefits and costs to society, there is a welfare loss, i.e. the extra benefit of producing a unit is greater than the extra cost and, therefore, society would benefit if the unit was produced
- there is likely to be productive inefficiency because the firm may not be producing at the output where average costs are minimised.

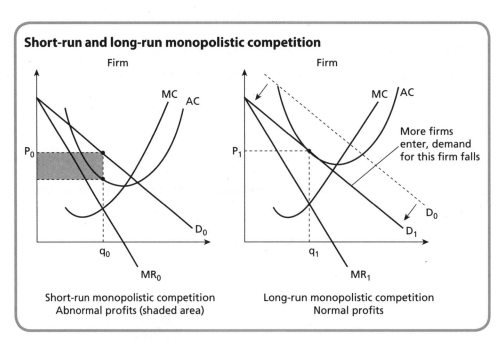

Short-run and long-run monopolistic competition

Short-run monopolistic competition
Abnormal profits (shaded area)

Long-run monopolistic competition
Normal profits

In monopolistic competition, individual firms want to boost their own demand. To do this they will use **non-price competition**, such as:

- advertising
- branding
- loyalty cards
- additional services, such as home delivery or delivery and installation.

Price Discrimination

Price discrimination occurs when a producer charges different prices for the same product. This is also called **third degree price discrimination**.

For example, the price paid for a plane ticket, a hotel room or car insurance will vary according to when they are purchased.

For price discrimination to occur:

- producers must have control over prices
- there must be markets with different demand conditions
- it must not be possible to move from one market to another (otherwise people would all buy in the low price market).

Ways of Separating Markets to Price Discriminate

Markets can be separated by:

- time, e.g. different prices for train tickets at peak times compared to the rest of the day or different hotel room prices at weekends compared to during the week
- age, e.g. lower prices for those over a certain age or free entry for young children
- distance, e.g. the cost of transport / delivery from the low-price market can be so high that it is not worth those in the high-price market going to the low-price market.

Price discrimination may occur due to imperfect information. For example, firms may be able to charge different prices for the same product because buyers in one market are not aware of what others are paying.

Price discrimination is often easier in the service industry because:

- you cannot easily resell a service (e.g. you cannot resell a haircut), so services cannot be bought in a low-price market and resold in a high-price market
- different consumers are prepared to pay different prices for the same service based on its value to them.

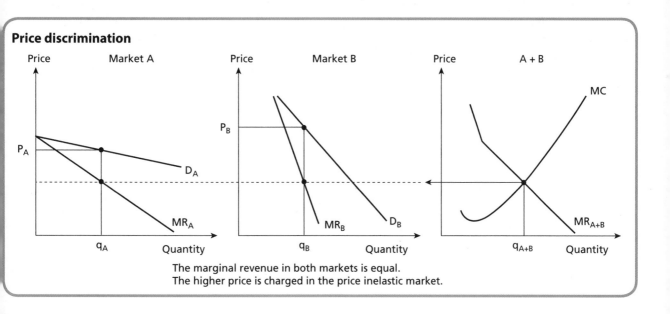

Price discrimination

The marginal revenue in both markets is equal.
The higher price is charged in the price inelastic market.

Price discriminators will:

- add the marginal revenues in the different markets together at each price (this is called horizontal summation)
- profit maximise where the combined marginal revenue equals the marginal cost
- produce in each market at this profit-maximising level, so the marginal revenue is the same in each market.

When price discrimination occurs, the price will be:

- higher in more price inelastic markets
- lower in more price elastic markets.

The marginal revenues will be equal to each other, so no extra revenue can be gained by selling more in any one market.

Disadvantages of Price Discrimination

The producer charges different prices for products and this reduces consumer surplus.

In perfect price discrimination, the producer charges exactly what the consumer is willing and able to pay – a different price is charged for every unit. This removes the entire consumer surplus.

Benefits of Price Discrimination

By price discriminating, businesses can earn greater revenue and profits. This means they may provide some products that would not be provided if a single price was charged.

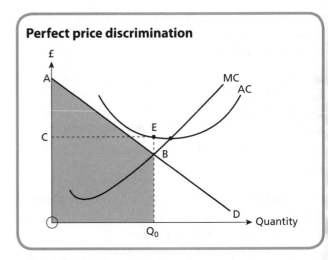

Perfect price discrimination

In the diagram:

- the firm is a perfect price discriminator, i.e. it charges a different price for every unit and the consumer pays exactly the price he or she is willing to pay
- there is no consumer surplus
- if the output is Q_0, the revenue for the business is A_0BQ_0O and the total costs are C_0EQ_0
- if the business only charged a single price of C, the revenue would be C_0EQ_0O.

With a single price, the revenue would not cover the costs and the product could not make a profit in the long run. However, with perfect price discrimination, the revenue does cover the cost and the firm can provide the product that would otherwise not be available.

SUMMARY

- In monopolistic competition, there are many firms and each firm faces a downward-sloping demand curve.

- In monopolistic competition, firms make normal profits in the long run due to market entry and exit.

- Price discrimination occurs when a different price is charged for the same product.

- Price discrimination requires markets to be separated, so a buyer cannot buy in the low-price market and resell in the high-price market.

- When price discriminating, a business charges a higher price when demand is price inelastic.

QUICK TEST

1. A firm in monopolistic competition faces a downward-sloping demand curve. True or false?

2. State **two** ways a firm can separate its markets to price discriminate.

3. Firms in monopolistic competition can make abnormal profits in the long run. True or false? Explain your answer.

4. Price discrimination occurs because of differences in costs. True or false?

5. In perfect price discrimination consumer surplus is maximised. True or false?

6. Profit maximising price discriminators have the same level of marginal revenue. True or false?

PRACTICE QUESTIONS

1. Explain why a firm might be able to charge different prices for the same product in different markets. **[15 marks]**

2. Discuss the view that price discrimination only benefits producers. **[25 marks]**

3. 'In monopolistic competition, firms cannot make abnormal profits.' Discuss. **[25 marks]**

Business Objectives

Traditional Theory of the Firm

In the traditional economics model, businesses are assumed to profit maximise. This occurs at the output where there is the biggest positive difference between total revenue and total costs.

Profit maximisation occurs when marginal revenue equals marginal cost. This is known as the **marginal condition**.

- If marginal revenue is greater than marginal cost, there is a profit on the additional unit and so overall profits increase when the unit is produced – more units should be produced.

- If marginal revenue is less than marginal cost, there is a loss on the additional unit and so overall profits decrease when the unit is produced – fewer units should be produced.

- If marginal revenue equals marginal costs, no more profit is made by producing another unit – profits are maximised.

Alternative Theories of the Firm

Although it is assumed that firms profit maximise, this may not always be the case in real life. Alternative theories of the firm consider other objectives.

Sales Revenue Maximisation

Sales revenue maximisation occurs at the output where marginal revenue equals zero. At this output, total revenue cannot increase further – it is maximised (Q_3 in the diagram on the bottom left).

By increasing sales, a business may increase its **market share**.

$$\text{Market share (\%)} = \frac{\text{sales of the business}}{\text{total market sales}} \times 100$$

With more market share, a business may have more power over suppliers and gain purchasing economies of scale.

Growth

Growth occurs at the highest output where no loss is made, i.e. the highest output (or where total revenue = total costs, shown by Q_4 on the diagram) at which average revenue is equal to average cost.

Satisficing

Herbert Simon argued that managers are trying to absorb huge amounts of information and deal with many different groups within the business (e.g. different departments), all of whom have their own objectives. This means that it may not be possible to maximise any one objective. Managers may have to reach a compromise that 'satisfices' the different groups.

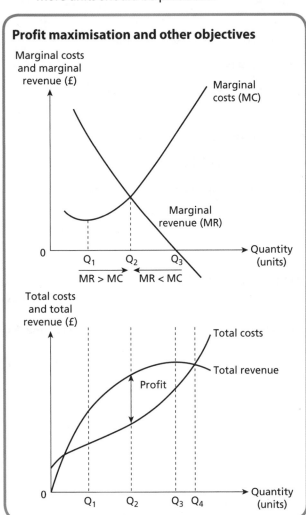

Profit maximisation and other objectives

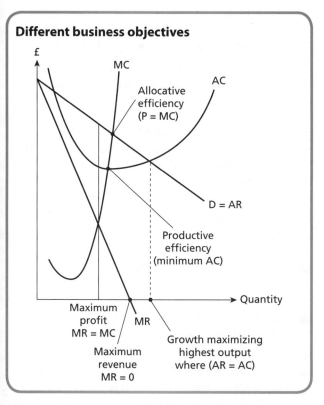

Different business objectives

- £
- MC
- AC
- Allocative efficiency (P = MC)
- D = AR
- Productive efficiency (minimum AC)
- Quantity
- Maximum profit MR = MC
- MR
- Maximum revenue MR = 0
- Growth maximizing highest output where (AR = AC)

The Divorce Between Ownership and Control

A 'divorce' between ownership and control occurs because the owners of a company are often not the ones actually managing the business.

The owners are likely to be investing in the business in return for financial rewards and they employ managers to generate these returns for them. However, if the managers have their own objectives, this can create problems.

Managers will have more information about the day-to-day running of the business, so shareholders may have to rely on them to look after their interests.

The danger is that managers do not maximise profits but pursue other objectives. For example:

- if their pay is linked to the size of the business, they may pursue growth
- if their pay is linked to revenue, they may try to maximise sales revenue.

This is why many firms give their senior managers shares in the business as part of the reward package – to encourage them to act in the shareholders' interests.

The owners of the business are called the **principal** and the managers are their **agent**. There are possible conflicts of interest in the principal-agent relationship.

The Size of a Business

The size of a business may be measured by:

- the value of sales
- the number of employees
- the number of outlets
- the total value of its assets
- the total value of its shares – this is called **market capitalisation**.

Market capitalisation = share price × number of shares

The size of a business should not be measured by profit – the profit is the outcome of the business activity, not a measure of size.

Motives for Business Growth

Some firms want to grow because by being bigger:

- they may benefit from internal economies of scale and lower unit costs
- they will have greater visibility in the market, which may help develop brand loyalty
- they will have more power over suppliers and can, therefore, determine delivery terms and quality.
- they may gain monopsony power.

Also, managers may measure their personal achievements in terms of how much they can grow the business.

How Businesses Grow

Businesses can grow by:

- **organic** or **internal growth**, i.e. when a business grows by selling more of its products
- **external growth**, i.e. when one business joins with another – this is called **integration**.

Integration can take the form of:

- a **merger**, where two or more businesses join together to create a new business
- a **takeover** (or acquisition), where one business gains control of another, e.g. by buying the majority of its shares.

Types of integration include:

- **horizontal integration** – where one business joins with another at the same stage of the same process, e.g. one bank joins with another bank, possibly to gain internal economies of scale
- **vertical integration** – where one business acquires another at a different stage of the same process:
  - **forward vertical integration** – where a business joins with another at a stage nearer the customer, e.g. a manufacturer buys a retailer, possibly to gain control of supplies
  - **backward vertical integration** – where one business joins with another at a stage nearer the source of the products, e.g. a manufacturer acquires a supplier, possibly to guarantee access to the market
- **conglomerate** – where one firm joins with another in a different production process, possibly to spread risks by operating in more than one market.

Constraints on Growth

There are many reasons why businesses might not grow:

- to avoid internal diseconomies of scale, such as communication, coordination and control problems
- because they lack funds for growth
- the owners may prefer to keep the business small (rather than bring in outside investors or grow it to the point where a large management team are required) to keep it under their control
- government regulation may prevent a firm from getting too big in a market, e.g. the actions of the Competition and Markets Authority.

External growth can bring many problems because the firms involved have different ways of doing things:

- employees may have different values (e.g. quality vs low cost or short-term vs long-term profits), which can lead to a clash of cultures, resulting in friction, resentment and staff leaving
- different processes and systems may not work well together.

Retrenchment

Retrenchment occurs when businesses get smaller.

A business may decide to pull out of certain markets or close certain stores to focus on the more profitable aspects of the business.

One form of retrenchment is **demerger**. This occurs when businesses that have joined together through takeovers and mergers decide to separate and become separate business again. It could be because of diseconomies of scale or intervention by the regulatory authorities.

By demerging:

- a business may avoid diseconomies of scale (however it may be losing internal economies of scale)
- a business may become more profitable, e.g. by selling off the less profitable parts
- a business may raise money from asset sales
- consumers may get lower prices if unit costs fall due to fewer diseconomies of scale
- employees will be affected by the sale – it may lead to fewer jobs if the smaller business needs fewer managers / coordinators / communications staff.

SUMMARY

- In traditional economics, it is assumed that firms profit maximise (where MR = MC).
- Alternative theories of the firm include sales maximisation and growth maximisation.
- A divorce between ownership and control means that those running the business on a day-to-day basis are not the owners. The owners and managers may have different objectives.
- Growth can be internal and external.
- External growth may be horizontal, vertical or conglomerate.
- A demerger occurs when a business splits into separate parts.

1. What is the profit-maximising level of output?

2. What is the revenue-maximising level of output?

3. What is the highest level of output a firm can produce at without making a loss?

4. What is meant by 'satisficing'?

5. The sales of a business are £20 000. Total sales in the market are £50 000. What is the market share of the business?

6. If one food producer joins with another food producer, it is called:

    A   horizontal integration.

    B   conglomerate integration.

    C   vertical integration.

    D   organic integration.

7. What is meant by 'forward vertical integration'?

8. What is meant by 'conglomerate integration'?

9. State **two** ways of measuring the size of a business.

10. What is meant by the 'divorce between ownership and control'?

PRACTICE QUESTIONS

1. Explain the differences between internal and external forms of growth.   [10 marks]

2. Discuss whether horizontal integration is a better form of growth than vertical integration.   [15 marks]

Competition, Technology and Efficiency

Competition

The degree of competition in a market will depend on factors, such as the number of firms in an industry and how they compete with each other.

Competition is generally regarded as desirable because:

- it increases the choices available to consumers
- it provides an incentive for firms to innovate and become more efficient
- it provides an incentive for firms to improve the quality of what they are offering.

Competition takes different forms. For example:
- competing on price
- competing with the product or service itself
- competing with additional services provided, e.g. free delivery, installation or guarantees.

Contestable Markets

A **contestable market** exists when there are low barriers to entry and exit, so new suppliers are able to enter the market and compete. This market has existing competition and it is possible for other firms to enter.

In a perfectly contestable market:

- there are no costs to entry or exit
- there is perfect information
- there are no **sunk costs** (costs that a business is already committed to and cannot be recovered)
- the new entrants have access to the same production techniques as the established firms.

Barriers to contestability in a market will occur if there is:

- brand loyalty to established firms, i.e. customers are reluctant to switch to new competitors
- economies of scale for established firms, so smaller, new entrants would be uncompetitive in terms of average cost (e.g. a high MES)
- legal protection, such as patents, i.e. the existing provider is legally protected and new entrants could not provide the same product

- the need for licences, e.g. to operate in a particular area or offer a particular service
- the provision of a good or service by the government and a regulation that it cannot be provided by others
- protectionist measures, e.g. quotas or tariffs for foreign goods and services
- control of suppliers, e.g. through vertical integration, so that new entrants cannot easily get access to resources
- control of resources or technology.

Sunk costs are costs that a business is already committed to and, therefore, cannot be recovered. For example, a business might:

- face high redundancy costs if it closed down
- worry about the damage to its brand reputation if it stopped producing and withdrew from the market
- have invested heavily in branding, marketing, research and development
- have machinery or IT systems that cannot easily be sold and used elsewhere.

If sunk costs are high, a business will lose large sums of money if it leaves the industry. This creates more pressure to compete and stay. Existing firms will respond aggressively if another firm tries to enter the industry, which is likely to deter new entrants.

Hit-and-Run Competition

The lack of barriers to entry in contestable markets means that businesses from outside the industry may come in to benefit from abnormal profits and then leave when they have been competed away. This is known as 'hit-and-run' competition.

For example, an item may become fashionable and profitable. This attracts others into the industry to provide a similar offering. When the item becomes less fashionable, the businesses move on to find other sectors with abnormal profits.

Existing firms may keep prices lower (e.g. using limit pricing) to reduce the threat of hit-and-run entry.

Making Markets More Contestable

Governments may try to make markets contestable to encourage competition and innovation by:

- deregulating markets to allow more firms to compete, e.g. allowing more firms to offer bus services, taxi services or airline services
- encouraging entrepreneurs, e.g. offering financial incentives for start-ups, to challenge the existing providers
- reducing barriers to entry, e.g. removing protectionist measures.

Competition Policy

Competition policy is government policy aimed at protecting consumers and businesses from abuse by dominant firms. It aims to ensure that firms do not act against the public interest. For example, it protects consumers against monopolies, cartels and restrictive practices.

In the UK, the main competition authority is the **Competition and Markets Authority (CMA)**. This organisation aims to promote competition for the benefit of consumers and make markets work well for businesses and the economy.

The responsibilities of the CMA include:

- investigating mergers that could restrict competition
- conducting investigations in markets where there may be competition and consumer problems
- investigating where there may be breaches of UK or EU restrictions against anti-competitive agreements or abuses of dominant positions
- bringing criminal proceedings against individuals who commit the 'cartel offence'
- enforcing consumer protection legislation to tackle practices and market conditions that make it difficult for consumers to exercise choice.

Regulators

In addition to the CMA, the government has appointed bodies in many industries to regulate behaviour (e.g. price increases) and ensure there is sufficient competition. These include:

- OfCom – regulates telecommunications industry
- OfGem – regulates the office of gas and energy markets
- OfWat – regulates the water services
- ORR – the Office of Rail and Road.

Efficiency in Markets

Allocative Efficiency

Allocative efficiency is analysed by considering the extra (marginal) benefit of a unit to society compared to the extra costs to society of providing it.

Allocative efficiency occurs at the output where the **social marginal benefit (SMB)** is equal to **social marginal cost (SMC)**.

Assuming the consumer is fully informed and appreciates the full social benefits of the additional unit, the price paid should reflect the social marginal benefit.

The extra cost of producing a unit is known as the marginal cost. Assuming this reflects the full costs to society of providing the unit, it will reflect the social marginal cost. (In reality, if the external costs of an activity are not taken into account in the free market, it may reflect the private marginal cost rather than the social marginal cost.)

- If the SMB of a unit is greater than the SMC, society's welfare will increase if the unit is produced.
- If the SMB of a unit is less than the SMC, society's welfare will decrease if the unit is produced.
- If the SMB of a unit equals the SMC, society's welfare cannot increase if another unit is produced – it is maximised. At this level of output, there is allocative efficiency.

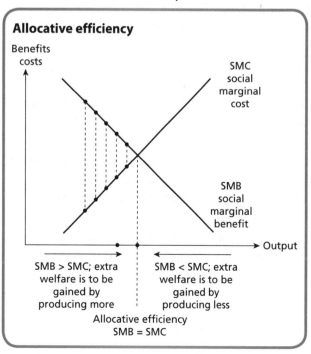

Allocative efficiency

Benefits costs

SMC social marginal cost

SMB social marginal benefit

Output

SMB > SMC; extra welfare is to be gained by producing more

SMB < SMC; extra welfare is to be gained by producing less

Allocative efficiency
SMB = SMC

Productive Efficiency

Productive efficiency occurs when a business is producing at the level of output at which average costs are minimised – the cost per unit cannot be lower. The business has benefited from all the internal economies of scale without incurring diseconomies of scale.

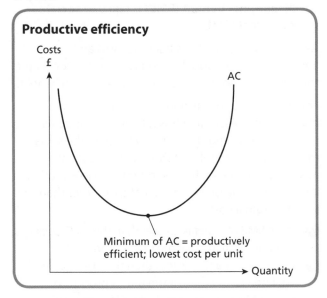

Productive efficiency

Costs £

AC

Minimum of AC = productively efficient; lowest cost per unit

Quantity

Static efficiency occurs when there is the most efficient combination of resources at a given moment in time.

Dynamic efficiency refers to changes in efficiency over time. Efficiency can improve over time with:

- better working practices
- improvements in management practices
- research and development
- investment in human and non-human capital
- new technology and technological change.

Dynamic efficiency may involve a trade-off. For example, to invest in better technology may involve higher costs in the short run. However, without this investment and innovation, the firm may be unable to improve over time.

Dynamic efficiency will occur when there is an incentive to improve and where there is the capability and funds available to do so.

Efficiency and Market Structures

	Allocative efficiency	Productive efficiency	Dynamic efficiency
long-run equilibrium perfect competition	yes	yes	may not be incentive to innovate
long-run equilibrium monopoly	no	no	may use abnormal profits to innovate

X-inefficiency was described by Liebenstein and occurs when there is little incentive for a firm to control its costs.

For example, in a monopoly where there are barriers to entry, a business may not keep costs as low as possible. This means that costs may be higher than they would be in a more competitive market.

X-inefficiency may occur if:

- employees are not managed effectively, so they are not as productive as they could be
- managers do not seek out the lowest cost suppliers.

Technology

Technology refers to the application of scientific knowledge for practical purposes.

Technology can change the way products are produced. For example, there is much more flexibility even in mass production these days, e.g. you can design aspects of your car to personalise it. This is known as mass customisation – it is mass production, but the cars are customised to meet individual requirements.

Technology is important to the creation of new processes, e.g. new methods of production that can improve the output in relation to inputs (improve productivity) and reduce the unit costs (improve efficiency).

Technology is important to the development of new products. For example, smartphones, tablets and virtual reality headsets are all relatively new – these new markets have been created by technological advancements.

Technology can destroy existing markets and is, therefore, a threat to some producers. For example, technology has made typewriters all but obsolete and the growth in smartphone sales has affected sales of watches and maps.

Technological change can affect:

- the total levels of production – more may be produced with better technology
- productivity, e.g. self-service checkouts can help each member of staff to be more productive (higher output per worker)
- efficiency – with better technology, the unit costs can be lower due to fewer mistakes being made and fewer employees being required for a given task.

Invention occurs when there is a new idea, i.e. a discovery.

Innovation occurs when this idea is successfully developed and launched in the market. Innovation creates demand.

The term **creative destruction** was introduced by Joseph Schumpeter. It describes how the abnormal profits earned by monopolies act as an incentive for others to be innovative – other firms will innovate (be creative) to remove (destroy) the existing monopoly and gain their own abnormal profits. Therefore, monopolies encourage innovation.

SUMMARY

- A contestable market exists when there are low barriers to entry and exit, so new suppliers are able to enter the market and compete.
- Sunk costs are costs that a business has already committed to and cannot be recovered.
- Competition can be an incentive to innovate and improve the quality of the goods and services provided.
- Allocative efficiency occurs when social marginal benefit equals social marginal cost.
- Productive efficiency occurs at the output where average costs are minimised.
- Dynamic efficiency occurs if efficiency increases over time.
- Innovation occurs when new ideas are successfully developed.

QUICK TEST

1. What is meant by 'dynamic efficiency'?

2. What is the difference between innovation and invention?

3. Allocative efficiency occurs when:

   A $SMB = SMC$

   B $SMB > SMC$

   C $SMB < SMC$

   D $SMB + SMC = STB$

4. What is meant by a 'contestable market'?

5. Productive efficiency occurs at the minimum of:

   A total costs.

   B average costs.

   C average revenue.

   D total revenue.

6. What is a sunk cost and why does it matter?

7. What is meant by 'creative destruction'?

8. What is meant by 'technology'?

9. Give **two** ways in which technology can affect businesses.

10. State **two** ways in which greater competition can affect a market.

PRACTICE QUESTIONS

1. Explain the benefits to consumers if a market is contestable. **[15 marks]**

2. Explain why lack of competition is likely to lead to allocative and productive inefficiency in monopoly markets. **[15 marks]**

3. Evaluate the view that competitive markets are more efficient than monopoly markets. **[25 marks]**

The Labour Market

Labour

Labour is a factor of production. In a market economy, employees are paid wages. Wage rates are determined by the supply of and demand for labour – they represent the price of labour.

The Demand for Labour

Labour is demanded because it produces output that can be sold and generates revenue.

The demand for labour is derived from the demand for the final good or service, i.e. labour is demanded because the products that it produces are demanded. If demand for the products increases, the demand for labour will increase.

The demand for labour will be downward sloping because as more employees are hired, the marginal product will fall (due to the Law of Diminishing Returns). The marginal revenue from selling their output is either constant (in perfect competition, as each unit is sold at the same price) or falls as more units are sold and the price has to be lowered to generate the demand. This reduces the value of extra workers' output.

The demand curve for labour shows the quantity of employees demanded at each wage rate, all other factors unchanged.

A business demands that employees generate output that is worth more or at least equal the wage rate. As the wage rate falls, there are more employees who generate output worth more than or equal to the wage rate and so the quantity demanded of labour increases.

A change in the wage rate leads to a movement along the demand for labour curve. A change in other factors leads to a shift in the demand for labour.

- At wage W_0, the number of employees who generate output worth more than or equal to the cost of employing them is L_0.
- At lower wages, there are more employees who generate output worth more than or equal to the wage rate.
- At $W_1 L_1$ employees will be demanded.

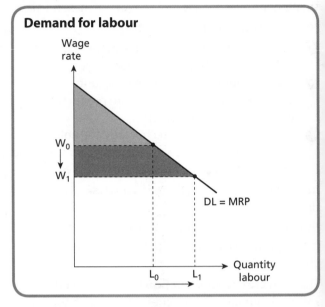

Demand for labour

The demand for labour will shift if:

- labour becomes more productive, e.g. because of more training, better organised work (e.g. specialisation), the use of more capital, the use of more or better technology, or better management
- the demand for the final product increases, e.g. due to an increase in income for normal products, a fall in the price of a complement, an increase in the price of a substitute, or better marketing activities.

The **wage elasticity of demand** shows how sensitive the quantity demanded of labour is to wage changes.

Wage elasticity of demand

$$= \frac{\text{percentage change in quantity demand of labour}}{\text{percentage change in wage rate}}$$

- If demand is wage inelastic, a percentage change in wages leads to a smaller proportionate change in the quantity demanded of labour. The wage elasticity has a value (ignoring the sign) of less than 1.
- If demand is wage elastic, a percentage change in wages leads to a bigger proportionate change in the quantity demanded of labour. The wage elasticity has a value (ignoring the sign) greater than 1.

Example

A 10% increase in wages reduces the quantity demanded of labour by 20%.

Wage elasticity of demand $= \dfrac{-20\%}{+10\%} = -2$

The value (ignoring the sign) is 2, which is wage elastic.

Any proportionate change in wages has 2 times the effect in percentages on the quantity demanded of labour.

Example

A 10% increase in wages reduces the quantity demanded of labour by 2%.

Wage elasticity of demand $= \dfrac{-2\%}{+10\%} = -0.2$

The value (ignoring the sign) is 0.2, which is wage inelastic.

Any proportionate change in wages has 0.2 times the effect in percentages on the quantity demanded of labour

The wage elasticity of demand will depend on:

- how easy it is to replace employees with other factors of production (e.g. replace staff with computers) – the easier it is, the more wage elastic demand will be
- what proportion of total costs wages represent – the bigger the proportion, the more an increase in wages affects costs and the greater the fall in the quantity demanded is likely to be.

The Supply of Labour

The supply of labour shows the number of employees willing and able to work at each wage in a given industry all other factors unchanged. This is usually upward sloping. As the wage rate increases, there are more people willing and able to work in this industry.

The supply of labour at any wage rate depends on:

- the wages available elsewhere – the more attractive wages are elsewhere, the lower the supply may be in this industry (depending on how easy it is for people to switch from one industry to another)
- non-monetary characteristics of the job, e.g. the working environment, the hours and the risk – if the work is messy, unpleasant and at unusual hours, the supply is likely to be less

- the skills needed – the more qualifications or skills needed, the lower the supply will be
- the number of people willing and able to work – this will be affected by the tax and welfare system, legislation on the working age, birth and death rates and **net migration**.

Net migration measures the difference between the number of people coming into the country and the number leaving the country over a given period.

The Labour Market

In a free market, the wage rate should adjust to bring equilibrium in the labour market.

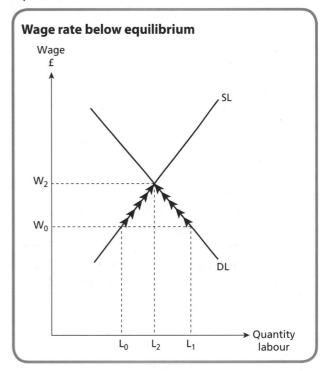

If the wage rate is below equilibrium:

- there is excess demand for labour (L_0L_1)
- the wage increases
- the quantity supplied of labour increases
- the quantity demanded is reduced until equilibrium is reached at W_2L_2.

If the wage rate is above equilibrium:

- there is excess supply of labour
- the wage decreases
- the quantity supplied of labour decreases
- the quantity demanded increases until equilibrium is reached.

Equilibrium Wage

If demand is high and supply is low, the equilibrium wage will be high compared to a market in which demand is low and supply is high.

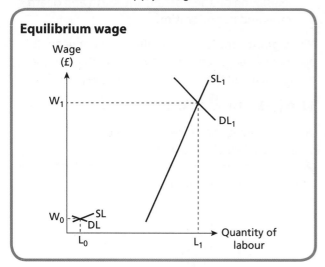

Equilibrium wage

An Increase in Demand for Labour

An increase in the demand for labour should lead to an increase in the equilibrium wage rate and number employed. The impact on wages compared to employment depends on the wage elasticity of supply. The more wage inelastic supply is, the more wages will increase compared to jobs.

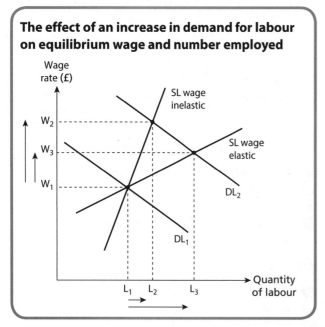

The effect of an increase in demand for labour on equilibrium wage and number employed

An Increase in the Supply of Labour

An increase in the supply of labour is likely to lead to lower wages and higher employment. The impact on wages relative to employment depends on the wage elasticity of demand. The more wage inelastic demand is, the more wages fall relative to employment.

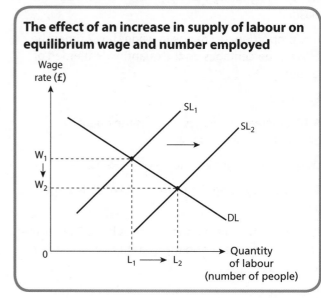

The effect of an increase in supply of labour on equilibrium wage and number employed

Change in the supply or demand of labour	Impact on equilibrium wage and quantity of labour
(assuming a downward-sloping demand curve and an upward-sloping supply curve)	
increase in demand for labour	• higher wages • higher equilibrium quantity
decrease in demand for labour	• lower equilibrium wage • lower equilibrium quantity
increase in supply of labour	• lower equilibrium wage • higher equilibrium quantity
decrease in supply of labour	• higher equilibrium wage • lower quantity

SUMMARY

- The labour market is made up of the demand for and supply of labour.

- The demand for labour is a derived demand.

- The demand for labour is determined by the productivity of the workforce and revenue of the output produced.

- The wage rate is the price of labour.

- The wage rate adjusts to bring equilibrium in the labour market.

- The wage elasticity of demand measures how sensitive demand for labour is to changes in the wage rate.

QUICK TEST

1. Why is labour a derived demand?

2. What is meant by the 'marginal revenue product'?

3. What brings about equilibrium in the labour market?

4. State **two** factors that might increase the demand for labour.

5. State **two** factors that might increase the supply of labour.

6. What is the likely impact of an increase in the demand for labour on the equilibrium wage?

7. What is the likely impact of an increase in the supply for labour on the equilibrium wage?

PRACTICE QUESTIONS

1. Explain the effect of an increase on demand on the wage rate in a market.   [10 marks]

2. Explain why wages differ in different labour markets.   [10 marks]

Wage Differentials

A **wage differential** occurs when wage levels differ between different labour markets.

If all jobs were perceived as being equally desirable and there was not immobility between labour markets, wages would be the same for different occupations.

If earnings in Industry A were lower than in Industry B, employees would leave the low paid sector (A) and move into the high paid sector (B). This would increase the supply in Industry B and bring down the wage level.

In theory, employees would move around until wages were equal in all markets.

However, in reality, wage differentials exist for a number of reasons:

- **occupational immobility** – differences in the skills required mean it may not be possible for employees to move into another industry easily

- **geographical immobility** – employees may not be able to move from one region to the next, e.g. due to prohibitive costs, such as differences in house prices or high transport (commuter) costs
- **information problems**, e.g. employees do not realise what vacancies are actually available
- **non-monetary aspects of the job**, e.g. if the job is dangerous, involves unattractive working conditions or unsocial hours, it may not attract labour even if wages are higher because of these differences
- **discrimination**, e.g. women may be paid less than men for the same work – this is illegal under the Equal Pay Act but does occur.

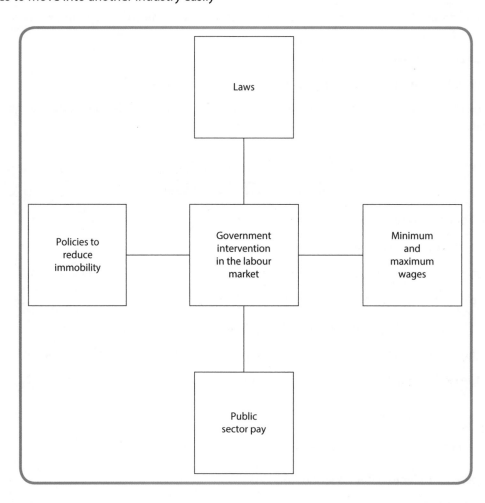

Government Intervention in the Labour Market

The government intervenes in the labour market to protect employees from exploitation.

There are many employment laws that affect redundancy, dismissal, maternity, sick pay, pensions and holidays and give employees some protection.

A current labour market issue is zero-hours contracts. Employees might have a contract with an employer to work for them and not others but are guaranteed zero hours of work – the employer employs the employee as and when there is demand. This creates uncertainty for the employee and means earnings are unknown, which can create problems with financial planning.

There are also discussions over whether people who deliver for companies, such as Uber or Deliveroo, are employees or self-employed, which affects their entitlement to various legal rights.

The government also intervenes to set a minimum wage in the labour market.

The National Minimum Wage

The **National Minimum Wage (NMW)** provides a minimum legal level for wages in any market.

If the minimum wage is set above equilibrium, there will be excess supply – the quantity of labour demanded is less than the quantity supplied.

A national minimum wage increases the earnings of those in work but may lead to more unemployment.

The overall effect on employees' earnings depends on the wage elasticity of demand for labour – if this is very elastic, an increase in wages leads to a much bigger proportionate fall in the quantity demanded and so overall earnings of employees may fall.

The effect of the NMW

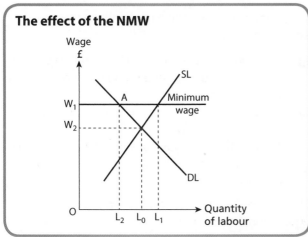

- The minimum wage is set at W_1.
- At this wage rate, the quantity supplied is relatively high at L_1.
- The quantity demanded is L_2.
- There is excess supply of labour at $L_2 L_1$.
- Total earnings of the workforce is $0 W_1 A L_2$.

The introduction of a minimum wage may affect employees' motivation and lead to higher productivity. This could shift the demand curve for labour outwards and lead to higher employment and total earnings.

The **National Living Wage (NLW)** is a legal minimum that must be paid to anyone over 25.

Maximum Wage

The government could also set a maximum wage it if it was trying to limit pay increases:

- If the maximum wage is above the equilibrium wage rate in the market, there will be no effect
- If the maximum wage is below the equilibrium wage rate in the market, there will be excess quantity demanded in the market.

Maximum wage

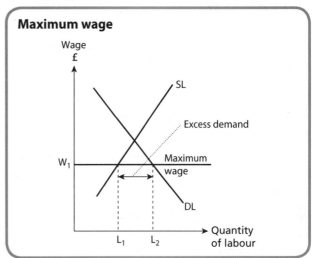

- At W_1, the quantity demanded is L_2 and the quantity supplied is L_1.
- There is excess demand at $L_2 L_1$.
- In a free market, there will be upward pressure on wages.

The government might invest in training to improve skills in the public sector.

Public Sector Pay

The government is a big employer in the UK. This means that the pay awards in the public sector (such as in the NHS and education) can have a big influence in terms of costs and prices. They also set a level that private sector firms might take into account. Therefore, the pay in the public sector might influence wages generally in the economy.

Government Policies to Improve Labour Mobility

To help improve mobility between labour markets the government might:

- invest in training to improve skills
- provide relocation allowances to help people move to where the jobs are
- intervene in the housing market, e.g. to provide affordable housing for low-paid employees wanting to move to expensive areas
- provide better information and advice services to help people find work and get jobs.

Trade Unions

Trade unions are organisations that represent employees and protect the rights of the workforce.

Unions can act to:

- push up wages, potentially above the equilibrium
- restrict supply by insisting on certain skills and qualifications for someone to do a specific job.

If, by being a member of a trade union, employees feel more secure and motivated, it might increase productivity and shift demand for labour outwards. This can lead to more wages and employment.

Unions may also work with management to develop better working practices and methods, increasing productivity and demand for labour.

'Sticky' Wages

Wages may be 'sticky' (slow to change) because employees may:

- have contracts that last for a fixed period of time, e.g. a year, so the wage cannot legally be changed in this period
- resist any attempt to reduce wages, e.g. either individually, or as part of a trade union, they may threaten to take industrial action (withdraw their labour and strike) to make employers keep wages as they are.

This means the labour market may not be in equilibrium at any moment.

QUICK TEST

1. What is meant by a 'wage differential'?

2. What is meant by 'occupational immobility' of labour?

3. What is meant by 'geographical immobility' of labour?

4. What is the purpose of the National Minimum Wage (NMW)?

5. If a minimum wage is above the equilibrium wage, what is the impact on the quantity of labour demanded and supplied?

6. How might a trade union affect wages?

7. What is wage discrimination?

8. State **two** non-monetary aspects of a job.

PRACTICE QUESTIONS

1. Explain the possible effect of an increase in the National Minimum Wage.   **[15 marks]**

2. To what extent can the different earnings of different occupations be explained by market forces?   **[25 marks]**

Income, Poverty and Wealth

Income is a flow concept. It shows the flow of earnings going to factors of production over a given period of time, usually a year. It includes wages, rental income, profits and interest from savings.

The flow of income earned in an economy over a year is measured by **gross domestic product (GDP)**.

Wealth is a stock concept. It shows the stock of assets belonging to a person, business or economy at a given moment in time. It includes shares and property.

Income vs Wealth

If you took a snapshot of everything a person owns, minus what they owe, this is their wealth. It might include a car, a flat and other possessions. These could have been bought at any time in their life.

If you measure a person's salary for that year, this is their income.

Someone who is not earning but has a lot of assets has a high wealth and low income.

Income equality measures how income is distributed within an economy.

Reducing the inequality within an economy (i.e. the difference between those with high incomes and low incomes) is often a government objective, as this is considered 'fair'.

Just because reducing inequality is considered fair, does not mean it is economically efficient and vice versa. A labour market could be efficient and lead to some people earning far more than others – this may not be seen as fair or good for society.

If incomes are very unequal, it may lead to social unrest, as those with less are unhappy with those who have far more.

The **Gini coefficient** measures the degree of income or wealth inequality in an economy.

The higher the coefficient, the greater the degree of inequality.

In the diagram there is a line of absolute equality. On this line, the bottom 10% of income earners have 10% of the income, the bottom 20% have 20% of the income, etc. Income is equally divided in society.

The line of actual income distribution is the **Lorenz curve**. This shows what proportion of the country's income the bottom 10%, 20%, etc. of income earners actually have. For example:

- the bottom 30% of income earners have only 15% of the country's income
- the bottom 70% of income earners have only 50% of the country's income.

The Gini coefficient measures the size of the area between the line of actual distribution and the line of absolute equality compared to the total area below the line of absolute equality.

The Gini coefficient has a value from zero to one, where:

- 0 = everyone has the same income (absolute equality)
- 1= one person earns all the income in the economy.

The bigger the coefficient, the further the line of actual distribution is from the line of absolute quality and the more unequal distribution is.

Causes of Income and Wealth Inequality

Inequality can occur for a variety of reasons. For example, it might be because of:

- differences in the availability and standard of education, plus its cost (e.g. the level of tuition fees) – education can affect a person's ability to earn and the amount they can earn
- unemployment levels – those unemployed will be on low earnings
- differing pay rates in the economy, especially the existence of low paid jobs

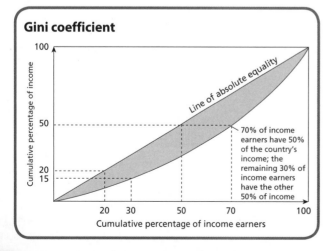

Gini coefficient

Cumulative percentage of income (y-axis): 100, 50, 20, 15

Line of absolute equality

70% of income earners have 50% of the country's income; the remaining 30% of income earners have the other 50% of income

Cumulative percentage of income earners (x-axis): 20, 30, 50, 70, 100

- the inheritance of assets by some individuals, creating wealth for them and potentially earning them an income (e.g. a house that can be rented out)
- differences in pensions, e.g. a state pension is likely to be relatively low, whereas some workplace pensions are significantly higher.

Achieving Greater Income Equality

There are different ways that a government can achieve greater income equality within a country.

Redistribution of Incomes
Incomes can be redistributed via greater benefits and / or a progressive tax and benefits system.

Greater Benefits
Greater benefits might be:

- **contributory benefits**, such as pensions and jobseeker's allowance, where individuals or employers make a contribution into the National Insurance Fund
- **non-contributory benefits**, such as housing benefit, carer's benefit and child support, which do not require a contribution to have been made – individuals simply qualify for them. To be paid these benefits, individuals must pass tests to see if they require them (this is called *means testing*).

A Progressive Tax and Benefits System
A progressive tax and benefits system occurs when the marginal rate of tax increases as income increases. Higher income earners pay proportionately more tax and welfare benefits are redistributed to those on lower incomes. This reduces income inequality.

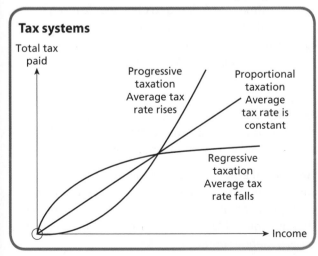

Tax systems

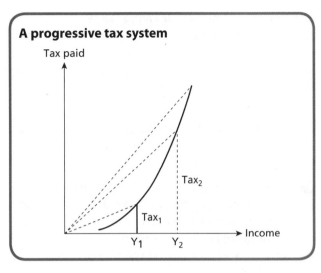

A progressive tax system

In a progressive tax system:

- as income increases, the marginal rate of tax increases
- the average rate of tax increases as income increases due to the increased marginal rates
- average tax paid per £ $= \dfrac{\text{total tax paid}}{\text{income}}$
- the average rate of tax is shown by the gradient of the dotted lines at each level of income; as income increases, the dotted lines get steeper.

However, a progressive tax and benefit system can have adverse effects. It might:

- reduce the incentive to work, as people may not want to start working and having to pay tax
- create **moral hazard** – individuals may not look for ways to improve their ability to work because the state provides for them as they are.

In addition to benefits, a government might help low earners in other ways:

Indirect Taxes
Indirect taxes, e.g. VAT, are regressive taxes. Whatever a person's income, he or she must pay the same amount of VAT. For low-income earners, this will represent a higher proportion of their income than for high-income earners. Therefore, by reducing indirect taxes, the government will help the low-income earners proportionately more than the high-income earners.

The National Minimum or Living Wage

The National Minimum Wage prevents wages for the low paid being as low as they would be in the free market. Therefore, in theory, it helps to reduce the gap between low and high incomes.

Increasing Employment

One of the main causes of poverty is unemployment. The government can, therefore, try to increase employment through policies, such as:

- fiscal and monetary policies, e.g. increased government spending or lower taxation rates, to boost aggregate demand or lower interest rates to stimulate borrowing and spending
- retraining schemes to help people get back into work.

Poverty

Absolute poverty is defined by the United Nations as 'a condition characterised by severe deprivation of basic human needs, including food, safe drinking water, sanitation facilities, health, shelter, education and information. It depends not only on income but also on access to services.'

It occurs when incomes fall significantly below the level required to live a modest but adequate existence. Obviously, the decision about what is 'modest and adequate' is a value judgement (a matter of opinion) and society's views may change over time.

Relative poverty occurs when individual or household income falls below the national average or median income. The official measure of relative poverty in the UK is where household income is less than 60% of median income.

Overall poverty, as defined by the United Nations, takes various forms, including:

- a lack of income and resources to ensure that citizens have sustainable livelihood
- hunger and malnutrition
- ill health
- limited or lack of access to education
- increased mortality through sickness
- homelessness and unsatisfactory housing
- social discrimination.

It is also characterised by citizens of a country having a lack of participation in making decisions that affect them economically, socially and culturally.

Forms of Poverty

Poverty can occur in all countries in different forms:

- mass poverty in many developing countries
- areas or regions of poverty within otherwise developed countries
- sudden poverty due to disaster or conflict.

The Effects of Poverty

Poverty can lead to:

- a loss of status and income
- a decline in people's self-respect
- health issues
- a sense of social exclusion, creating social conflict.

Causes of Poverty

The main causes of poverty include:

- long-term unemployment (some unemployment may be short term as people are simply between jobs – this is less of an issue)
- low pay, e.g. due to discrimination or a lack of a minimum wage in the economy
- homelessness
- addiction, affecting health and employability.

How to Reduce Poverty

Government policies to reduce poverty include:

- changes to the taxation and benefits systems, e.g. increasing tax credit for working families
- increases in the National Minimum Wage
- changes in indirect taxes, e.g. taxing luxury goods heavily
- encouraging start-ups to promote business growth
- policies to create more jobs
- the provision of free services, e.g. education
- investment in training to give people more skills (but these take time to take effect)
- subsidies for certain services, e.g. childcare to enable people to take a job.

Equity vs Equality

Equality occurs when goods and services are distributed equally. **Equity** refers to fairness. What is regarded as 'fair' is a value judgement.

Horizontal equity occurs when individuals in the same financial position are taxed in the same way. For example, everyone in the same income tax band pays the same rate of tax – there is no discrimination on the basis of gender or race.

Vertical equity occurs when people in different financial circumstances are taxed differently. For example, there is a tax free allowance so low-income earners pay no tax. However, as income increases, those in higher tax bands have higher amounts of income taxed at higher tax rates.

A **poll tax** is a tax which is a fixed sum of money per person. Everyone pays the same sum of money in tax so this meets the criteria of horizontal equity (e.g. everyone earning £20 000 a year would pay the same amount of tax) but would not meet the criteria of vertical equity (because the tax would be a higher proportion of their income for low-income earners than it would be for high-income earners).

SUMMARY

- **Income is a flow concept.**
- **Wealth is a stock concept.**
- **Absolute poverty is measured by the ability of an individual to achieve a certain level of existence.**
- **Relative poverty occurs when an individual's earnings fall a certain amount below the median.**
- **The Gini coefficient is a measure of income and wealth inequality.**
- **A progressive tax system occurs when the marginal rate of taxation increases as income increases.**

QUICK TEST

1. What is meant by 'income'?
2. What is meant by 'wealth'?
3. What is meant by 'relative poverty'?
4. What is meant by 'absolute poverty'?
5. State **two** effects of poverty.
6. State **two** possible causes of poverty.
7. Give **two** policies that could be used to reduce poverty.
8. Which of the following measures income inequality?

   A the multiplier

   B the accelerator

   C the Gini coefficient

   D the retention ratio

9. With reference to the data in the table, which of the following statements is true?

	Gini coefficient
Country A	0.1
Country B	0.9

   A The distribution of income in Country A is more equal than in Country B.

   B 10% of the population of Country A have 100% of the income.

   C 10% of the population of Country A have 90% of the income.

   D The wealth distribution in Country B is more equal than in Country A.

PRACTICE QUESTIONS

1. Explain why income inequality exists in the UK. **[15 marks]**

2. Evaluate the most appropriate policies that the government could adopt to reduce income inequality in the UK. **[25 marks]**

3. Evaluate whether the free market is likely to lead to income equality. **[25 marks]**

Public and Private Ownership

Markets

Markets occur when there are buyers and sellers and the forces of supply and demand operate.

Market forces can lead to competition and, as businesses compete against each other, this can result in:

- relatively low prices
- an incentive to innovate
- an incentive to improve the quality of service.

All of the above benefit the consumer.

If there are no market failures, competitive industry markets can be allocatively and productively efficient, as in perfect competition.

However, in reality, there are market failures and imperfections, such as monopolies, information problems and production and consumption externalities. These failures may mean that the government will want to intervene to regulate markets and improve the way they work.

Government intervention could involve:

- direct intervention, such as nationalising an industry
- providing more information to overcome information gaps
- legislating or regulating, e.g. competition policy to control monopoly power.

Public Ownership

Public ownership occurs when the government has control of an organisation. For example, the UK government controls:

- Companies House
- Land Registry
- Meteorological Office
- Ordnance Survey
- Student Loan Book
- Nuclear Decommissioning Authority.

Nationalisation occurs when assets are transferred from the private sector to the public sector. For example, the UK government took control of the Royal Bank of Scotland in the financial crisis.

Public Sector Organisations

Organisations that are owned by the government rather than the private sector:

- may have social objectives and can be less profit focused than private sector organisations
- can help with employment, creating jobs and reducing poverty
- can provide relatively high wages for employees, reducing poverty
- can avoid the problems caused in the free market, e.g. take account of external costs and benefits
- can protect strategic industries, e.g. defence
- can protect 'a way of life', e.g. farming
- can be used to control pay increases in the economy and help reduce cost push **inflation**
- could generate profits for the government.

Potential Disadvantages of Public Sector Ownership

Organisations in the public sector may not be open to the same market forces as a private sector organisation. Therefore, public sector organisations:

- may be x-inefficient due to a lack of pressure from private owners to keep costs down
- may be productively inefficient because they can be monopolies
- may mean consumers suffer from higher prices and poor quality services due to lack of competition and innovation
- may experience moral hazard, e.g. if there is a belief that the government will always ensure the survival of the organisation, it may affect behaviour and lead to excessive risk taking or inefficiency
- may be used for political gains rather than to achieve economic efficiency, e.g. to win votes in a region by subsidising an industry even if the industry is inefficient
- may lack an incentive to be efficient and innovate, e.g. if profits are taken and used in other industries.

Privatisation

Privatisation occurs when assets are transferred from the public sector to the private sector.

In the UK, privatisation has led to a major reduction in the size of the public sector as a proportion of **gross domestic product (GDP)** and employment. Government-owned organisations now produce less than 2% of GDP and are responsible for less than 1.5% of total employment.

Major privatisations in the UK have included Associated British Ports; British Aerospace; British Airports Authority; British Airways; British Coal; British Energy; British Gas; British Petroleum; British Rail; British Steel Corporation; British Telecom; London Underground; Rolls Royce; Royal Dockyards; Royal Mail; Thomas Cook; and Water Industry.

Forms of privatisation include:

- denationalisation, i.e. transferring ownership from the public sector to the private sector by selling shares
- deregulation, i.e. introducing competition into what were restricted markets – it may involve removing barriers to entry to allow more firms in, e.g. removing a monopoly or allowing more competition
- contracting out, i.e. allowing private sector firms to tender for contracts, such as school lunches or waste collection
- private finance initiatives (PFI) involving the public and private sectors working together, e.g. the private sector builds a road, which is used by government for number of years, so the private sector can then charge a fee.

Possible Benefits of Privatisation
Transferring assets to the private sector:

- means the government can raise revenue from the sale and from tax on the profits of the privatised organisations
- may mean the government does not have to subsidise a loss-making organisation any more
- creates more shareholders in the economy and more interest in business
- makes managers accountable to shareholders, potentially putting greater focus on efficiency and profit

- provides incentive to increase competition and improve efficiency, as the managers and owners can keep the rewards.

Criticisms of Privatisations in the UK
Some commentators argue that:

- some assets have been sold off too cheaply and could have raised more money (e.g. Royal Mail)
- some privatisations have simply replaced government monopolies with private ones that now need regulating
- the pressure for profits may lead to short cuts when it comes to safety, e.g. on railways.

The **Single European Market (SEM)**, which the UK belonged to as part of the European Union (EU), has led to more deregulation (or **'market liberalisation'**). The Single Market promotes the free movement of goods, services, financial capital and labour.

Government Intervention in Markets

To reduce or prevent market failures and imperfections the government may intervene in markets.

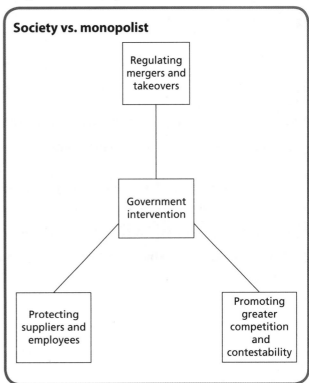

Society vs. monopolist

Regulating mergers and takeovers

Government intervention

Protecting suppliers and employees

Promoting greater competition and contestability

For example, the government may regulate:

- monopoly power, e.g. railways operating on a given line – it may take actions, such as restricting price increases, ensuring certain quality and performance standards are met, and regulating the profits that are made
- any proposed mergers or takeovers that could create monopoly power (through the Competition and Markets Authority)
- any potential price fixing or cartels in a market
- the promotional activities of businesses to ensure consumers receive appropriate information to make well-informed choices, e.g. through the labelling regulations on food, and are not misled
- the quality and safety standards that businesses must meet, e.g. in relation to employment
- the way businesses deal with other businesses, including suppliers.

The government may also encourage competition:

- by encouraging start-ups
- through restricting monopoly and monopsony power
- by deregulating markets.

The aim of government intervention is to lead to:

- more efficiency
- lower prices
- more choice
- better quality.

The effectiveness of government intervention will depend on:

- the quality of information it has – it can be difficult for the government to run or regulate a business or industry as it will not have as much information as those involved in the business on a day-to-day basis, i.e. there is asymmetric information
- whether **regulatory capture** occurs.

Regulatory capture occurs when the regulators start to favour those that they are supposed to be regulating. By working closely with managers and businesses in industry, the government regulator may start to associate with their causes.

It is a market failure when the regulator promotes the interests of the industry rather than the public interest.

SUMMARY

- **Governments may intervene to reduce market failures and imperfections.**
- **There are different forms of intervention, such as taxing, subsidising, directly providing or regulating.**
- **Governments may intervene to protect groups, such as suppliers and employees, to increase competition or to regulate takeovers and mergers.**
- **Nationalised industries are run by the government and may have social objectives.**
- **Privatised organisations are state-owned assets that have been transferred to the private sector.**

1. What is meant by 'nationalisation'?

2. What is meant by 'privatisation'?

3. State **two** possible reasons for nationalisation.

4. State **two** possible problems of public sector ownership.

5. State **two** possible reasons for privatisation.

6. What is 'regulatory capture'?

7. What is meant by 'deregulation'?

8. State **two** ways in which a government may intervene in a market.

9. State **two** ways in which a government may encourage greater competition in a market.

10. What is 'monopoly power'?

PRACTICE QUESTIONS

1. Explain why a government may wish to nationalise an industry.   **[15 marks]**

2. To what extent is privatising industries economically desirable?   **[25 marks]**

Macroeconomic Policy Objectives

Macroeconomics focuses on the economy as a whole, rather than individual markets.

Studying the price level in one market is an example of **microeconomics**. Studying the average price level in the economy is an example of macroeconomics.

An **objective** is a target. It is usually:

- quantifiable (expressed as a number)
- time specific (set to be achieved by a given date).

A **policy** is a way of trying to achieve a target. Governments use policies, such as **fiscal policies** (involving government spending and changes to tax and benefit systems) and **monetary policies** (involving changes in interest rates) policies, to achieve its objectives. The typical macroeconomic objectives of a government are:

Economic growth

This is measured by an increase in national income. Generally the government will want economic growth so that its citizens are earning more. Higher income per person is usually associated with a higher standard of living.

Low unemployment

This is a measure of how many people are able and willing to work at the given wage rate but are not in employment. The government will want low levels of unemployment as it is a waste of resources and socially undesirable. If people are employed, it should provide them with a better standard of living and help economic growth.

Stable prices

If prices are changing unpredictably, it is difficult for firms to plan investment and households to plan how much they will spend and how much they want to or need to save. Stable prices enable better planning and give businesses and households more confidence in the government's control of the economy.

A healthy trade position

The trade position measures the difference between the value of exports and imports. If a country is buying in heavily from abroad, this suggests that its businesses are uncompetitive. If it is selling far more abroad than it is buying in, the other governments may want to take action to protect their own industries. A government will aim for a sustainable trade position.

Some of these objectives may work well together, e.g.:

- economic growth can help create jobs and reduce unemployment
- stable prices may make trade more appealing and help a country's trade position.

However some objectives may be difficult to achieve at the same time. For example:

- increased spending to reduce unemployment may lead to higher prices
- higher economic growth may lead to more spending on imports and worsen the trade position.

Other economic objectives of government may relate to:

- environmental targets, e.g. reducing carbon emissions and reducing global warming
- income distribution, e.g. reducing inequality and poverty
- balancing its budget, e.g. ensuring its income covers its spending.

These objectives may conflict with other objectives:

- faster economic growth may have negative environmental effects
- higher taxes on high-income earners to improve income equality may deter entrepreneurs and lead to slower economic growth.

Output Gaps

The **output gap** in an economy measures the difference between the actual level of national output and the potential output. The potential output of an economy is the maximum level of output that could be achieved while maintaining stable inflation over a given time period. This depends on how many people are available to work and how many hours they are willing to put in (labour); the number of buildings, machines and equipment that is available to work with (capital); and the efficiency with which resources can be combined (productivity). It is usually expressed as a percentage.

A **negative output gap** occurs when the actual output is below the potential, i.e. the economy is operating below its potential. Some resources, such as capital, are underutilised, which is likely to increase unemployment. More unemployment will put downward pressure on prices and this in turn will put downward pressure on costs and prices.

A **positive output gap** occurs when the actual economy is above the potential. The economy is producing more than is sustainable in the long term given existing resources and technology, e.g. employees are working overtime. This will put upward pressure on prices and is inflationary.

Government Policies and Output Gaps

If there is a negative output gap, the government may try and boost demand in the economy using reflationary policies, such as lower tax rates, increased government spending on final goods and services, and lower interest rates. This can boost aggregate demand.

If there is a positive output gap, the government may try to reduce aggregate demand using deflationary policies, such as higher tax rates, less government spending on final goods and services, and higher interest rates. The government might also use supply-side policies to increase the potential output.

Item	To reduce aggregate demand	To increase aggregate demand
interest rates	increase to encourage savings	decrease to encourage borrowing and investment
taxation rates	increase to reduce disposable income and profits	decrease to increase disposable income and profits
government spending on final goods and services	reduce	increase

Why is Low Unemployment a Government Objective?

Unemployment:

- can lead to inequality
- is a waste of resources leading to an economy operating within its **production possibility frontier**
- can cause individuals to feel dissatisfied and underutilised, which can lead to social unrest and affect votes
- reduces income tax revenue and increases welfare payments, which increases the budget deficit.

If the economy has unemployment and is operating below its potential output, the economy is wasting resources and will be operating within the PPF.

SUMMARY

- **Government objectives include high levels of employment, economic growth, a healthy trade position and stable prices.**

- **Some objectives may be achieved simultaneously, but some may conflict, e.g. to achieve lower unemployment may involve demand-side policies than pull up prices (at least in the short term).**

QUICK TEST

1. Give **two** typical macroeconomic objectives.

2. Explain **one** possible conflict between macroeconomic objectives.

3. Explain why a positive output gap may be inflationary.

PRACTICE QUESTIONS

1. Explain why low unemployment is a key objective of economic policy for many governments. **[15 marks]**

2. Discuss whether reducing unemployment should be the main objective of government. **[25 marks]**

The Phillips Curve

The **Phillips curve** shows a potential trade-off between **inflation** and unemployment.

An important aspect of the Phillips curve is the **non-accelerating inflation rate of unemployment (NAIRU)**. This is an estimate of the level of unemployment at which the labour market is in equilibrium with no pressure on inflation to change, because there is neither downward pressure on wages (because of high levels of employment) nor upward pressure on prices (due to low levels of unemployment).

A short-run Phillips curve is drawn for a given level of inflationary expectations.

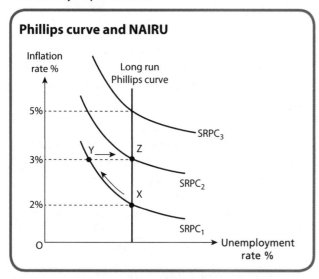

Phillips curve and NAIRU

If employees expect 2%, the relevant Phillips curve is SRPC$_1$. This means that if wages and prices are growing at 2% and this is the rate expected by employees, the economy will be in equilibrium at the NAIRU at X.

Similarly, if expectations were 3% and wages and prices were growing at 3%, the economy would be W on SRPC$_2$.

Moving Along a Short-Run Phillips Curve
Imagine the economy is at X with prices and wages growing at 2% and this is the expected rate of inflation with the economy in equilibrium. If aggregate demand now increases:

- there will be more demand for labour if aggregate demand increases
- the greater demand for employees will lead to firms competing for workers and trying to poach from other businesses
- this in turn will lead to higher wages and higher training costs as businesses have to take on more staff that require training
- prices increase due to the higher costs to protect profit margins
- as a result, unemployment does fall below the NAIRU but inflation is higher than 2%.

Alternatively, if aggregate demand fell:

- there would be less demand for goods and services and less demand for labour
- the fall in demand for labour would decrease wages and costs
- unemployment would rise above the NAIRU and inflation would fall below 2%.

The Long-Run Augmented Phillips Curve
Milton Friedman did not agree with the idea of a trade-off between inflation and unemployment in the long run. He believed there was no long-run trade-off and the long-run Phillips curve was a vertical line.

For example, if the economy is in equilibrium with inflation at 2% and employees expect inflation to continue to be 2%, they will base their wage bargaining on this rate. If the government then uses expansionist policies in the economy that create more demand and pull up prices, inflation may now increase, e.g. to 3%.

This means that if employees are still getting a 2% wage increase, with prices rising at 3%, the real wage has fallen. In real terms, employees are cheaper and this leads to an increase in the quantity demanded and a fall in unemployment.

Over time employees will realise that prices are growing at 3% and will demand this rate of pay increase. Once wages start growing at 3%, the same as prices:

- the real wage returns to its original levels
- employees become as expensive as they were before
- the economy moves back to the long-run equilibrium level of unemployment except that prices are now growing at 3% – they are on a new short-run Phillips curve.

If the government continues to use expansionist policies and inflation rises to 5%:

- if employees are being paid 3%, in real terms they are cheaper
- the quantity demanded increases again
- employees eventually appreciate inflation is 5% and push up their nominal wages restoring the real wage to its original level
- unemployment returns to its long-term equilibrium level but expectations are now on SRPC$_3$.

Reducing Inflation
Imagine the economy is in equilibrium, with prices and wages growing at 5%. This is the expected rate of inflation and the economy is at NAIRU. If the government introduces deflationary policies to reduce demand and reduce the rate of inflation, in the short term, employees are more expensive.

If inflation is 3% but wages are still growing at 5%, employees are more expensive and fewer will be demanded – unemployment will rise.

Over time:

- the higher rates of unemployment will put downward pressure on wage rate growth
- wages will start to grow at 3% in line with inflation
- the economy will return to its long-run equilibrium with prices now growing at 3%
- expectation will adjust to be 3% and the economy will be on the SRPC$_2$.

If the government continues to deflate the economy and prices start to grow at 1%:

- with wages still growing at 3%, employees will again be expensive
- unemployment will rise
- over time the higher levels of unemployment mean that wage growth should slow and come back in line with inflation at 1%.

Short-Run and Long-Run Phillips Curve

In the long run, the economy should adjust and return to the NAIRU whatever the rate of inflation. There is no trade-off between inflation and unemployment.

In the short run, however, there may be a trade-off, as money wages do not change at the same rate as inflation. This is because:

- employees may take time to realise what inflation actually is
- employees may be locked into pay contracts for a number of months or years
- wages are particularly sticky downwards, as employees are reluctant to accept lower money wage increases even if prices are growing more slowly.

Therefore, the short-run Phillips curve suggests:

- there is a short-run trade-off as wages grow at different rates from inflation
- unemployment can be brought down below its long-run equilibrium level if inflation continues to grow faster than wages

- attempts to reduce inflation will increase unemployment until wages start to grow at a slower level.

The key question is: 'how long is the short run?' Monetarists and classical economists believe the labour market adjusts relatively quickly and, therefore, it does not take long to get back to the NAIRU. If the government tries to stimulate demand with expansionist policies, assuming the economy was at NAIRU to start with and the economy adjusts quickly, these expansionist policies will lead to more inflation but no fall in unemployment. The government would be better focusing on supply-side policies to reduce the NAIRU.

The NAIRU can be reduced by:

- improving the mobility of labour
- increasing training
- improving productivity
- reducing trade union power to enable the labour markets to function more efficiently.

SUMMARY

- The Phillips curve shows a potential relationship between inflation and unemployment. However, in the long run when the labour market has fully adjusted, there may be no trade-off.

- NAIRU is the non-accelerating rate of inflation.

- In the short run, money wages may be 'sticky', e.g. because of wage contracts; this means the real wage may not be at the long run equilibrium rate.

- Keynesians believe the labour market is slow to adjust; classical economists believe it adjusts quickly.

1. What does NAIRU stand for?

2. What is the relationship between inflation and unemployment on the short-run Phillips curve?

3. What is the relationship between inflation and unemployment on the long-run Phillips curve?

4. Explain why a negative output gap may be deflationary.

5. In the diagram, $SRPC_1$ and $SRPC_2$ are short-run Phillips curves. LRPC is the long-run Phillips curve.

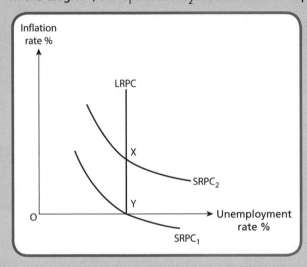

Which of the following would cause a movement from X to Y?

A	a fall in taxation	**C**	a cut in real interest rates
B	an increase in government spending	**D**	reduced inflationary expectations

PRACTICE QUESTIONS

1. Discuss whether it is possible for the government to keep unemployment below the NAIRU in the long run. **[25 marks]**

2. Evaluate the view that there is a trade-off between inflation and unemployment. **[25 marks]**

Short-Run and Long-Run Aggregate Supply

Aggregate Supply

The **aggregate supply** curve shows the amount of final goods and services producers in an economy are willing and able to supply at each price level in a given period.

The short-run aggregate supply curve shows the quantity supplied at each and every price before the factor markets, such as labour, have fully adjusted to any changes in price.

The long-run aggregate supply curve shows the quantity supplied at each and every price once markets have fully adjusted.

Economists differ in their views of how long it takes for an economy to move from the short run to the long run.

Short-Run Aggregate Supply (SRAS)

Each short-run aggregate supply curve is constructed for a given set of costs.

For example, an increase in money (nominal) wages will increase costs. At any price, firms will produce less. The short-run aggregate supply shifts inwards.

A decrease in money wages will cause costs to fall and the aggregate supply shifts outwards – at each price, more can be supplied.

The Short-Run and Long-Run Effect of a Decrease in Aggregate Demand

Money (nominal) wages are the wages paid. **Real wages** show the purchasing power of money wages – they are money wages adjusted for inflation.

Imagine the long-run equilibrium is at E and the economy is at potential output Y. If there is a decrease in **aggregate demand** (e.g. due to a fall in exports or consumer confidence):

- the price level will fall
- with lower prices but the same money wages, real wages will increase
- employees are more expensive, so the quantity demanded of labour will fall
- the economy will end up at B in the short run.

The fall in demand has led to lower prices, higher real wages and higher unemployment – the economy is below it potential output.

In the long run, with higher than usual levels of unemployment:

- there will be downward pressure on wages
- when money wages fall, real wages are reduced back to the long-run equilibrium level
- the economy moves back to the long-run equilibrium at C with the same potential output but lower prices.

Therefore, in the short run, the fall in demand leads to more unemployment. In the long run, the labour market will adjust and return to equilibrium – the fall in demand will lead to lower prices but the same level of unemployment.

In the long run, the economy returns to its potential output – the long-run aggregate supply curve is vertical.

The relationship between inflation and unemployment in the short run and long run can also be shown on the short-run and long-run Phillips curves.

The Short-Run and Long-Run Effect of an Increase in Aggregate Demand

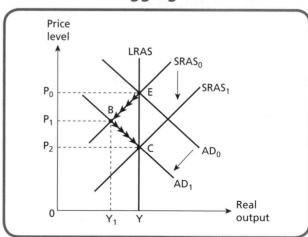

Imagine the long-run equilibrium in the economy is at point E. The economy is at its potential output given its existing resources. If aggregate demand increases (e.g. due to an increase in government spending):

- prices are pulled upwards
- assuming that money wages do not change, real wages will fall
- firms hire more labour and the quantity supplied in the economy increases
- the economy moves to point F with higher prices and output.

Firms are now producing above the economy's potential output. This means:

- there is excess demand for labour
- over time money wages are pulled up
- the increase in money wages increases costs
- aggregate supply shifts to $SRAS_1$
- the economy returns to equilibrium at G.

Over time the economy has returned to its potential output. Following the increase in aggregate demand, it has higher prices but the same level of output.

In the long term, the amount produced in the economy given its resource is Y_1 whatever the price. The long-run aggregate supply is vertical at Y_1.

In the short run, an increase in aggregate demand can reduce unemployment (with higher prices). However, in the long run, there is no trade-off between inflation and unemployment. This relationship between inflation and unemployment in the short run and long run can also be shown on the short-run and long-run Phillips curves.

Keynesians vs Classical Economists

Economists called **Keynesians** (named after the economist John Maynard Keynes) believe that the move from the short-run aggregate supply to the long-run aggregate supply is slow. They believe that money (nominal) wages are slow to adjust in the labour market so the real wage can stay above or below the long-run equilibrium for some time.

The reasons why money wages are slow to adjust include:

- money (nominal) wages may be fixed for some time due to contracts

- employees will be reluctant to take a cut in money wages even if prices are lower – there is a built in reluctance to accept lower money wages
- employees are slow to recognise changes in prices in the economy and, therefore, slow to accept appropriate adjustments in money wages. This is because employees buy a limited range of products and take time to appreciate what is happening to prices in general.

Keynesians argue that 'in the long run, we are all dead' and it is, therefore, important to focus on the short run and appropriate policies.

These mean, for example, that the economy could be 'stuck' at B. Rather than wait for the economy to adjust to C in the long run, the government may want to boost aggregate demand, e.g. through expansionist fiscal policy. This would pull up prices, reduce real wages and return the economy to long-run equilibrium with higher prices.

Classical economists believe that the labour market adjusts relatively quickly to the long-run equilibrium. If demand falls and prices fall, real wages will increase in the short run and increase unemployment. This excess supply of labour leads to downward pressure on wages, which will rapidly reduce money wages back to the long-run equilibrium level.

If demand increases and prices rise, real wages will decrease in the short run and decrease unemployment. The excess demand for labour will lead to upward pressure on wages, which increases money wages and brings the economy back to the long-run equilibrium level relatively quickly. Therefore, classical economists believe that the vertical long-run aggregate supply curve is the key when it comes to thinking about appropriate policies.

According to classical economists, increases or decreases in aggregate demand mainly affect prices, not output. Government policy should therefore focus on supply-side policies and shifting the long-run aggregate supply curve, e.g. focus on making markets more competitive and improving the efficiency of the labour.

The Effect of an Increase in Costs

Costs may increase due to external factors, such as increasing global energy prices or an increase in the price of imported products due to a fall in the exchange rate.

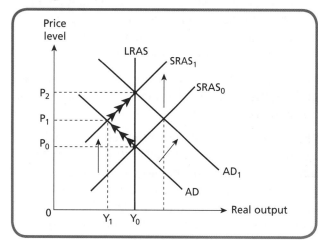

An increase in costs will mean:

- firms need a higher price for any given level of output (or less will be supplied at every price)
- the short-run aggregate supply curve shifts inwards
- the economy will move to P_1Y_1.

This means there are higher prices and lower output – this is called 'stagflation'.

If the government does nothing, according to classical economists, the economy will return to long-run equilibrium fairly quickly. The high levels of unemployment will put downward pressure on wages. This will reduce costs and the economy will return its equilibrium at the same price and unemployment level as before.

However, Keynesians would say that money wages will be slow to fall. This means real wages will be too high and there will be high unemployment for some time. In this case, the government might want to use reflationary measures to boost aggregate demand (to AD_1) to pull up prices and reduce the real wages again back to the long-run equilibrium level. The economy would end up with higher prices at P_2 and the same long-run level of unemployment.

Changes in the Long-Run Aggregate Supply (LRAS)

The long-run aggregate supply will shift if there is a change in the potential output of an economy.

This can happen for reasons, such as:

- changes in technology and the quantity and quality of capital
- changes in the quantity or quality of the labour force, e.g. changes to the retirement age or education system
- improvements in the way resources are managed and combined leading to an increase in productivity.

SUMMARY

- The aggregate supply curve shows the amount of final goods and services producers in an economy are willing and able to supply at each price level in a given period.
- The short-run aggregate supply curve shows the quantity supplied at each and every price before the factor markets, such as labour, have fully adjusted to any changes in price.
- The long-run aggregate supply curve shows the quantity supplied at each and every price once markets have fully adjusted.
- Real wages are money wages adjusted for inflation.
- Economists called Keynesians (named after the economist John Maynard Keynes) believe that the move from the short-run aggregate supply to the long-run aggregate supply is slow.
- Classical economists believe that the labour market adjusts relatively quickly to the long-run equilibrium.

1. What does an aggregate supply curve show?

2. Explain the difference between money wages and real wages.

3. What happens to real wages if prices rise and money wages stay constant?

4. Why might money wages be 'sticky' downwards?

5. What happens to the quantity of labour demanded if prices fall but money wages do not?

6. Explain the difference between the Keynesian and classical view of the labour market.

7. Explain why classical economists would focus on supply-side rather than demand-side policies to reduce unemployment.

8. Explain why Keynesian economists would focus on demand side rather than supply-side policies to reduce unemployment.

9. How might the long-run aggregate supply be made to shift outwards?

PRACTICE QUESTION

1. Discuss whether increasing aggregate demand is more likely to reduce unemployment or increase prices.   [15 marks]

Financial Markets

Financial markets exist to allow funds to move from those who have excess funds (more than they wish to spend) to those who have a shortage of funds (wish to spend more than their income). For example, some households may want to save whilst others want to borrow.

The linking of savers and borrowers can happen:

- directly through financial markets, when a company sells shares to investors or the government sells a bond to raise finance
- via **financial intermediaries** including banks, building societies, pension funds and insurance companies.

Types of Financial Market

Financial markets include:

Shares in a company usually give the owner a vote. A **shareholder** is a part owner of the business and usually there is one vote per share. Shares are also called **equity** and the sale and trading of shares happens on the **equity market**.

Bonds are IOUs sold by companies and the government. If businesses or governments sell IOUs, they are sold and traded on the **bond market**.

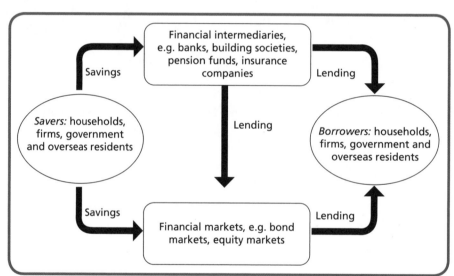

Global Financial Markets

The financial markets are enormous with vast amounts of money moving all over the world. For example, governments with surpluses may invest in UK company shares or government bonds. UK pension funds may buy shares all over the world.

These are truly global markets and world economies are interrelated. A shock in the financial markets of one economy will impact on others.

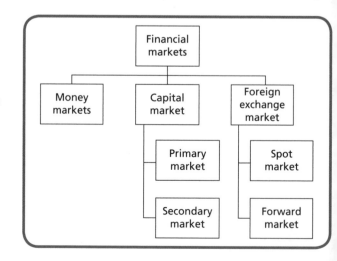

Money Market

The **money market** provides short-term finance to firms and the government. Money markets involve trading in short-term debt (with a maturity of less than 12 months), interbank lending (lending between banks) and short-term government borrowing through treasury bills.

Capital Market

The **capital market** provides medium to long-term finance.

Companies raise long-term finance by issuing shares and corporate bonds or through borrowing from banks. Companies will raise money for a variety of reasons, such as:

- takeover
- expansion
- investment in research and development.

Governments issue bonds (IOUs) to raise revenue.

Banks also raise money to support their lending by issuing bonds on capital markets.

The capital market is made up of:

- the **primary market**, which is when bonds and shares are sold for the first time
- the **secondary market**, which is when shares and bonds that already exist are traded. Stock exchanges exist to trade second-hand (already existing) shares.

The Foreign Exchange Market

The **foreign exchange market** (called 'forex') is the market in which different currencies are bought and sold.

The massive amounts of international trade flows that occur mean that businesses and governments need to convert funds from one currency to another. They do this in the foreign exchange market.

Foreign exchange (currency) can be traded on:

- the **spot market** – this involves the immediate changing of currency, i.e. the exchange rate if you change currency today
- the **forward market** – this involves setting a price at which to buy and sell currency at some point in the future. Forward markets are used by exporters and importers to protect themselves against possible movements in the exchange rate.

Debt and Equity Capital

Debt involves borrowing money that has to be repaid with interest. Loans and bonds are examples of debt.

The interest on debt is a fixed cost for the business (it is not related to the level of output). The interest must be paid before any dividends to the owners are paid out.

Government bonds are used to raise finance for a budget deficit. Corporate (company) bonds are used by businesses to raise finance. Most bonds pay a fixed rate of interest, which is called a **coupon**. Bonds usually have a fixed maturity date, which is the date when the issuer of the bond agrees to repay the initial sum borrowed.

Selling equity involves selling ownership in the business. Shares are equity. Shareholders can gain financially if their shares increase in value (but may lose money if the share price falls) and through profits being paid out as dividends. They also usually have a vote in what the business does.

Bond Prices, Market Interest Rates and Yields

The **yield** on a bond is the annual interest payment, or coupon, given as a percentage of the market price of the bond. It is the return earned on the bond by the bondholder.

$$\text{Yield (\%)} = \left(\frac{\text{coupon}}{\text{price of the bond}}\right) \times 100$$

If the coupon is a fixed annual amount:

- a fall in the market price of the bond will increase the yield
- a rise in the market price of the bond will cause the yield to fall.

Coupon per year (£)	Bond price (£)	Yield (%)
£5	£100	$\left(\frac{5}{100}\right) \times 100 = 5\%$
£5	£80	$\left(\frac{5}{80}\right) \times 100 = 6.66\%$
£5	£50	$\left(\frac{5}{50}\right) \times 100 = 10\%$
£5	£25	$\left(\frac{5}{25}\right) \times 100 = 20\%$

Example 1
When a bond is first issued, it has a coupon of £5 and a market price of £100, so the yield is 5%.

If the market rate of interest for other investments falls to 2.5%:

- the bond becomes very attractive to investors as it has a much higher return

- demand for bonds increases until the price reaches £200
- at this price the yield is $\left(\frac{5}{200}\right) \times 100 = 2.5\%$ and it is equal to what can be earned elsewhere
- at this point there is no incentive to buy bonds more than other investments as the returns are equal. (In reality, investors will accept different returns on assets depending on the degree of risk involved in holding them.)

Example 2
When a bond is first issued, it has a coupon of £5 and a market price of £100, so the yield is 5%.

If the market rate of interest for other investments rises to 10%:

- the bond is not very attractive to investors as it has a much lower return than the alternatives
- demand for bonds decreases and the price falls until the price reaches £50
- at this price the yield is $\left(\frac{5}{50}\right) \times 100 = 10\%$, which is comparable with the other investments.

The price of a bond will depend on:

- the appeal of bonds relative to other investments
- the risk of inflation, as this will reduce the value of the IOU when it is paid back
- the risk – this is generally relatively low for government bonds as governments generally pay their IOUs. However, in some cases they have not, so there is a risk. The greater the risk, the higher the return buyers will expect to compensate for it.

SUMMARY

- Debt involves borrowing money that has to be repaid with interest. Loans and bonds are examples of debt.

- The interest on debt is a fixed cost for the business.

- The money market provides short-term finance to firms and the government.

- The capital market provides medium to long-term finance.

- The foreign exchange market is the market in which different currencies are bought and sold.

QUICK TEST

1. What is the difference between a spot rate and a forward rate in the currency market?

2. What is a 'bond'?

3. The annual yield on a bond is 5% and the price of the bond is £50. What is the annual coupon?

4. Explain the difference between debt and equity capital.

5. What is the difference between the primary and secondary capital markets?

6. If the price of bonds increases, does the yield rise or fall? Explain your answer.

PRACTICE QUESTION

1. Explain the functions of the capital market.   [10 marks]

Banks and Risk

Commercial Banks

Commercial banks are the high street banks, such as Barclays, Lloyds, the Royal Bank of Scotland and HSBC.

The main functions of commercial banks are to:

- accept deposits from savers
- lend to households and firms
- provide efficient means of payment.

Commercial banks are a financial intermediary and play a key role in moving funds from those who have surplus funds (lenders / savers) to those who want those funds (borrowers).

Liquidity, Risk and Profit

Commercial banks want to make profits by lending.

Long-term lending is often the most profitable. However, the banks need to keep enough **liquid** (readily available) funds to quickly meet the requests of depositors who might want to withdraw their money.

Leaving money liquid and essentially sitting idle does not generate high returns. As a result, there is pressure on banks from their investors (who want profits) to use funds to lend long term and earn higher returns. Banks need to balance the need for short-term liquid funds for depositors and lending long term to earn high profits.

Banks also need to constantly consider the risk of the different forms of lending. Banks must try to balance their lending so they are not too exposed to people being unable to repay their loans.

Balance Sheet of a Commercial Bank

A bank's **balance sheet** provides a snapshot of its financial position at a given moment in time. It shows 'sources of funds' on one side (these are known as **liabilities** and **capital**) and 'use of funds' (its assets) on the other side. Liabilities are forms of borrowing. Capital includes money raised from shareholders and retained profit. Assets are items owned by the organisation. Given that every asset must have a source of funds to acquire it, total assets must equal total liabilities plus capital.

Liabilities can be split into:

- shareholders' funds – this is made up of funds from selling shares and the retained profits of the business

- money that the bank has borrowed from depositors or, for example, by issuing bonds.

Assets	Liabilities
cash (notes and coins)	issued share capital
balances held at the Bank of England	reserves (retained profits)
money at call and short notice (e.g. money borrowed from other banks via the interbank market)	long-term borrowing (e.g. bonds)
short-term borrowings (called commercial and treasury bills)	short-term borrowing
investments (e.g. holdings of shares and bonds)	deposits
loans and mortgages made to borrowers	
fixed assets (e.g. equipment and property)	

Credit Risk

Credit risk is the risk of a borrower being unable to repay what he or she owes to a bank. In this situation, the bank makes a loss.

If a loan is 'written off':

- the bank's assets are reduced
- an equivalent reduction is made to the other side of the balance sheet, by reducing the bank's capital (because the loss reduces the retained profits).

If a bank's capital is entirely reduced by losses, the bank becomes balance sheet insolvent.

Liquidity Risk

For a bank, a **liquidity risk** occurs if there is a danger that a large number of depositors and investors may withdraw their funds at once, leaving the bank short of funds. This is known as a 'run on the bank'. If a bank is unable to pay out to its depositors what they are owed, it is cash-flow insolvent. The failure of a bank can create financial instability because it can cause depositors and investors to assume that other banks will fail as well, which results in a run on more banks.

Credit Creation

Banks create credit by giving loans to their customers. Providing a loan, which is an asset to the bank, creates a corresponding liability for the bank in the form of a deposit in the customer's account.

If you deposit £100 in a bank:

- the bank may retain £10 (in case you ask for some of your funds) and lend £90
- the £90 may be spent and passed on to a business and its employees
- they deposit the money into their bank and £90 ends up back in the banking system
- the bank may then retain £9 and lend £81
- the £81 is spent and passed on to a business and its employees
- they deposit this in their bank, leading to another opportunity for more lending, and so on.

If 10% is retained at each stage, a £100 initial deposit will lead to deposits and **credit creation** of £100 + £90 + £81+ £72.9 + £…

The initial deposit has created a much bigger increase in the money supply due to credit creation.

Limits on Credit Creation

The limits on a bank's ability to create credit are:

- its holdings of capital and liquid assets
- the demand for credit
- the policy of the central bank.

A central bank, such as the Bank of England, can affect the demand for credit by, for example, changing the bank rate (the rate it charges the commercial banks).

It can also affect bank lending by changing required capital ratios (the amount of capital on a bank's balance sheet as a proportion of its loans) and by altering the value of liquid assets the banks must hold.

At the moment the Bank of England does not attempt to control bank lending by fixing or changing **reserve ratios** (how much banks must hold back in reserve from deposits). However in the United States, the Federal Reserve does specify reserve requirements with which the banks have to comply and, in 2019, the 'liquidity coverage ratio', introduced as part of the Basle III agreement, will be implemented in the UK.

Higher capital and reserve ratios mean that the banks' ability to create credit is likely to be reduced. If a bank's capital equals £5 billion and it is required to maintain a capital to loans ratio of at least 10%, the maximum value of the loans it can provide is £50 billion. If the capital to loans ratio is 50%, it could only create loans of £10 billion.

SUMMARY

- A reserve ratio is how much banks must hold back in reserve from deposits.
- A liquidity risk occurs for a bank if there is a danger that a large number of depositors and investors may withdraw their funds at once, leaving the bank short of funds.
- A bank's balance sheet provides a snapshot at a given moment in time of its financial position.

QUICK TEST

1. What is a balance sheet?
2. How might a higher reserve ratio affect credit creation?
3. Why do banks have to balance liquidity and profit?
4. What are 'assets'?
5. What is meant by a commercial bank?
6. What is meant by credit creation?
7. Explain what is meant by liquidity risk.
8. Explain what is meant by credit risk.

PRACTICE QUESTION

1. Explain the risks that banks face and how they might reduce them. **[10 marks]**

Types of Bank and Regulation

Investment Banks

An **investment bank** specialises in helping companies with their finances, e.g. to raise money, to undertake and finance a takeover and to advise them on share issues (what price they should be able to sell new shares at and when to offer them). It charges a fee for providing these services.

Investment banks are also involved in secondary markets; they buy and sell existing shares, commodities and foreign exchange for their clients and on their own behalf.

Commercial and Investment Banking Operations

Although, in the UK, several banks are both commercial and investment banks, the authorities are now introducing regulations to keep these activities separate.

This is because of the risks involved in using the deposits from the commercial part of the bank to invest in projects linked to the investment bank – it could put depositors' funds at unnecessary risk if they are used for high-risk projects for the investment arm.

The Vickers Report in the UK recommends that the commercial banking (or retail banking) activities of the banks are to be separated from investment banking activities. This means commercial deposits cannot be used by investment banks for trading. In 1993, the Glass Steagall Act in the US prevented commercial banks from carrying out investment banking and insurance business.

Other Institutions Operating in Financial Markets

Other types of financial institution that operate in UK and global financial markets include:

- insurance companies
- pension funds
- hedge funds
- private equity companies.

There is also something called the **shadow banking system** – this refers to financial intermediaries who are involved in providing credit across the global financial system, but who are not subject to regulatory oversight.

Regulation of the Financial System in the UK

In the late 1980s, the financial system in the UK was deregulated. These changes were called 'The Big Bang' and the aim was to make London a more attractive financial centre by making it easier to do business there.

This approach was known as 'light touch' regulation and has been blamed for much of the financial crisis that hit the UK (and the world) in 2008. It allowed banks to make very high-risk loans because adequate checks were not in place.

More recently, governments in many countries have introduced measures to regulate more closely and reduce the risks to the financial system because of the problems caused by high-risk lending in 2008 and the global recession caused by the financial crisis.

Financial Regulation

Economies and financial institutions in countries around the world are very closely linked to each other – a problem in one bank in one country can soon spread, because that bank is likely to have borrowed from other banks around the world.

The problems caused across the world by high-risk lending by banks in 2008 have led to much greater regulation of banks recently.

If banks fail, this can affect:

- savers who lose their funds
- businesses who cannot borrow
- governments who may decide to intervene
- taxpayers who may have to finance a bailout.

In the UK, in 2012, the **Financial Services Act** strengthened the role of the Bank of England in regulating the financial system. It established the **Financial Policy Committee (FPC)** and the **Prudential Regulation Authority (PRA)**, both of which are part of the Bank of England. It also set up the **Financial Conduct Authority (FCA)**, which works in conjunction with the FPC and PRA but is not part of the Bank.

The FPC is primarily responsible for **macroprudential regulation**, which is concerned with identifying, monitoring and removing risks that affect the stability of the financial system as a whole.

The PRA and FCA are mainly responsible for **microprudential regulation**, which focuses on ensuring the stability of individual banks and other financial institutions. It involves identifying, monitoring and managing risks that relate to individual firms.

The Financial Policy Committee (FPC)

The main objective of the FPC is to identify and monitor **systemic risks** to the UK financial system and take action to remove or limit them. Its secondary objective is to support the economic policy of the government.

Systemic risks are those that could lead to the collapse of the whole, or a significant part, of the financial system.

The FPC has two main powers:

- it can issue directions to the PRA and the FCA
- it can make recommendations to anyone, including the government.

The FPC has the power to make comply-or-explain recommendations to the PRA and FCA.

The Prudential Regulation Authority (PRA)

The PRA was established by the Bank of England as part of the Financial Services Act 2012. It is responsible for the regulation of around 1700 banks, building societies and other financial institutions.

The PRA has three objectives:

- to promote the safety and soundness of the firms it regulates
- to ensure there is an appropriate degree of protection for insurance policy holders
- to promote effective competition between the financial institutions.

The PRA is a regulator – it sets standards and policies that firms are expected to achieve. It also supervises and assesses the risk that firms pose in relation to the PRA's objectives. Where necessary, it takes action to reduce the risk.

The PRA:

- uses its judgement to determine whether financial firms are safe and sound
- assesses future risks as well as current risks
- focuses on issues and firms that pose the greatest risk.

Its aim is not to ensure there are no failures in the system (this could not be done), but to ensure that, if there is one, it does not cause significant disruption to the financial system.

The Financial Conduct Authority (FCA)

The aim of the FCA is to:

- protect consumers
- promote competition between the providers of financial services
- maintain a stable, resilient financial services industry.

The FCA uses its rule-making, investigative and enforcement powers to protect consumers and to regulate the financial services industry.

Problems of Financial Regulation

Some of the problems associated with financial regulation are:

- regulatory capture
- it might stifle innovation because financial institutions will avoid risk
- it might restrict the supply of credit to economic agents (households, firms or governments) who could make good use of additional funding
- it may lead to rapid growth in an unregulated shadow banking sector, which will generate even more risks.

Financial institutions exist to lend. If you overregulate one way of doing this, they might try to find another way.

Moral Hazard

Moral hazard occurs when people have an incentive to behave badly. For example, you may be likely to take greater risks if you are insured and know that a claim will be paid for by your insurance cover.

Moral hazard exists when an individual or organisation decides how much risk to take knowing, if things go wrong, someone else will bear a significant portion of the cost.

If there is a good chance that a bank will get emergency financial support from the government when it encounters problems, employees of the bank might be tempted to take increased risks.

The dilemma facing governments is that they do not want banks to fail but, if banks know the government will always intervene, they may take too many risks. This is why governments have tried to regulate banks more to reduce the risk. Governments have also tried to stop banks getting too big so, if one does fail, it does not bring down the whole financial system.

What is Systemic Risk?

A systemic risk occurs if there is a danger that problems with one bank could create problems for the whole industry or even the economy (there is a knock-on effect).

The global financial crisis in 2008 showed how much the world economy was at risk from problems in one specific sector.

Problems in the US banking sector started with high-risk lending, called the sub-prime market. This led to financial problems, not just in the US but in many different countries, as so many banks across the globe were linked to this form of lending.

Since the global financial crisis, the financial regulators in different economies have tried to make the banking system less vulnerable to reduce the risk created by individual banks. Banks now have various 'stress tests' they must pass to show that, even if they fail, they will not bring down the whole financial system.

Why Does Financial Stability Matter for the Economy?

According to the Bank of England, 'financial stability – public trust and confidence in financial institutions, markets, infrastructure and the system as a whole – is critical to a healthy, well-functioning economy.'

If the banking system fails:

- individuals may lose their savings
- firms may not be able to borrow and invest
- governments may not be able to finance their budgets.

Instability in the financial system can lead to:

- uncertainty and a fall in investment, which reduces aggregate demand and long-term supply in the economy
- uncertainty and greater savings by households and firms 'just in case', which reduces demand.

QUICK TEST

1. What is the difference between an investment bank and a commercial bank?
2. What is the role of the Prudential Regulation Authority (PRA)?
3. What is meant by 'moral hazard'?
4. What is the role of the FPC?
5. What is meant by 'systemic risk'?
6. State **two** reasons why financial stability matters for the economy.
7. What is meant by shadow banking?
8. What is an investment bank?

PRACTICE QUESTIONS

1. Explain how the UK financial system is regulated.   [15 marks]

2. To what extent does the UK financial system pose a risk to the UK economy?   [25 marks]

Money

Money is a type of IOU that will be accepted by other people in exchange for goods and services.

There are three main types of money in modern economies:

- currency
- bank deposits
- central bank reserves.

Each type of money represents an IOU from one sector of the economy to another.

Most money in the modern economy is in the form of bank deposits. These are created by commercial banks.

Functions of Money

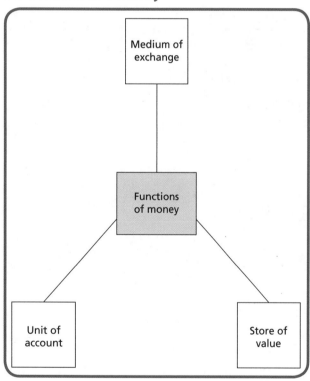

Money acts as:

- a store of value – something that is expected to retain its value in a reasonably predictable way over time
- a unit of account – the thing that goods and services are priced in terms of, e.g. on menus, contracts or price labels
- a medium of exchange – something that people hold because they plan to swap it for something else, rather than because they want the good itself.

Broad money is the money that consumers have available for transactions. It is made up of:

- currency, i.e. banknotes and coins, which are an IOU from the central bank, mainly to consumers in the economy
- bank deposits, which represents an IOU from commercial banks to consumers.

Broad money measures the amount of money held by those responsible for spending decisions in the economy (consumption and investment), i.e. households and companies.

Base (or central bank) money, is made up of IOUs from the central bank. It includes:

- currency, which is an IOU to consumers
- central bank reserves, which are IOUs from the central bank to commercial banks.

Base money is important because the central banks, who are the only issuers of base money, can implement monetary policy through it.

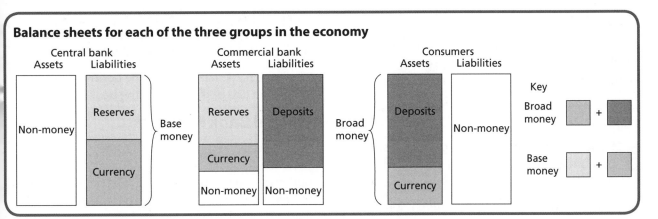

Balance sheets for each of the three groups in the economy

Balance Sheets

A **balance sheet** highlights the IOUs from different people to each other. Each IOU is a financial liability for one person that is matched by a financial asset for someone else (this is why it balances and is called a balance sheet).

- Broad money is represented by the sum of the dark-shaded and mid-shaded assets held by consumers.
- Base money is the sum of all of the mid-shaded and light-shaded assets.
- Each type of money features on the balance sheets of at least two different groups, because each is an asset of one group and a liability of another. If you own something (asset) the money must have come from somewhere (liability).

There are also lots of other assets and liabilities which do not fulfil the functions of money. Some of these are shown unshaded on the diagram above. For example, consumers hold loans, such as mortgages, which are liabilities of the consumer and assets of the consumer's bank.

Fiat Currency

Fiat currency refers specifically to banknotes and coins that are not convertible into another asset, such as gold. Currency is made up mostly of banknotes (over 90%), which are an IOU from the Bank of England to the rest of the economy.

Banknotes are a 'promise to pay' the holder of the note, on demand, a specified sum. This makes banknotes a liability of the Bank of England and an asset of their holders.

When the Bank of England was founded in 1694, its first banknotes were convertible into gold. This was known as the **gold standard**.

Since 1931, Bank of England money has been fiat money. Fiat money is accepted by everyone in the economy as the medium of exchange, although the Bank of England is in debt to the holder of its money. However, since 1931, that debt can now only be repaid in more fiat money – the Bank of England promises to honour its debt by exchanging banknotes for others of the same value forever.

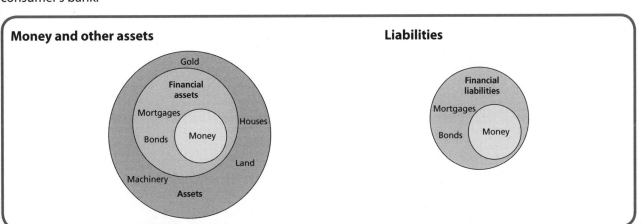

Money and other assets

Liabilities

Deposits

Currency (notes and coins) only accounts for a very small amount of the money held by people and firms in the economy. The rest consists of bank deposits.

Consumers generally do not want to hold much currency:

- for security reasons – it might get lost or stolen
- because money does not earn interest, whereas bank deposits often do.

Bank deposits can come in many different forms, e.g. current accounts or savings accounts held by consumers and some types of bank bonds purchased by investors.

For most household depositors, their deposits in banks are guaranteed up to a certain value. This means that customers remain confident in holding deposits and ensures that bank deposits can act as a medium of exchange.

Nowadays, bank deposits are often the main type of money. For example, most people now receive payment of their salary in bank deposits rather than in currency. Instead of changing those deposits back into currency, many consumers use them as a store of value and, increasingly, as the medium of exchange.

While currency is created by the Bank of England, bank deposits are mainly created by commercial banks.

Creating Deposits

The most significant element of creating deposits is through banks making new loans.

When a bank makes a loan to one of its customers, it credits the customer's account with a higher deposit balance. At that moment new money is created.

When the bank makes a loan, the borrower has also created an IOU of their own to the bank.

Central Bank Reserves

Commercial banks need to hold some currency to cover the frequent deposit withdrawals and other outflows. To allow this to happen, banks are permitted to hold a different type of IOU from the Bank of England – central bank reserves.

Central bank reserves are an electronic record of the amount deposited at the central bank, i.e. the amount owed by the central bank to each individual bank.

Reserves are a useful medium of exchange for banks, in the same way as deposits are for households and companies. If one bank wants to make a payment to another (as they do every day on a large scale when customers make their transactions), they tell the Bank of England who then adjusts their reserves balances, e.g. reserves are transferred from Barclays to HSBC.

The Bank of England also guarantees that any amount of reserves can be swapped for currency should the commercial banks require it. For example, if lots of households wanted to convert their deposits into banknotes on any given day, commercial banks could swap their reserves for currency to repay those households. As the issuer of currency, the Bank of England can make sure there is always enough to meet such demand.

SUMMARY

- There are three main types of money: currency, bank deposits and central bank reserves.
- Money acts as a store of value, a unit of account and a medium of exchange.
- Broad money is made up of currency (banknotes and coins) and bank deposits.
- Fiat currency refers to banknotes and coins that are not convertible into another asset.
- Base money, or central bank money, is made up of IOUs from the central bank.

QUICK TEST

1. What are the **three** main types of money?
2. Why is money a store of value?
3. Why is money a medium of exchange?
4. Why is money a unit of account?
5. What is meant by 'broad money'?
6. What is meant by 'base money'?
7. What is 'fiat money'?
8. How are deposits created?
9. What are central bank reserves?
10. What was meant by 'the gold standard'?

PRACTICE QUESTION

1. Explain the functions of money.   **[15 marks]**

Central Banks and Monetary Policy

The Bank of England is the UK's **central bank**. It is owned by the government but is responsible independently for monetary policy.

The main responsibilities of the Bank of England are:

- issuing banknotes and managing the UK's currency
- providing monetary stability – the Bank's **Monetary Policy Committee (MPC)** has the objective of delivering stable prices and aims to achieve this by setting interest rates
- providing financial stability – the **Financial Policy Committee (FPC)** aims to reduce risks in the financial system and the Bank intervenes to manage failing financial organisations if necessary.

The Bank is banker to the government. However, this role has declined in recent years. The Debt Management Office (DMO) now issues gilts on behalf of the Treasury and has taken over responsibility for issuing treasury bills and managing the government's short-term cash needs.

The Bank acts as a lender of the last resort to the banking system. This can involve:

- the regular provision of liquidity as and when banks needs funds, because of customers withdrawing money and the bank needing to cover this on some days
- emergency provision of liquidity to a bank if it has cash flow problems
- emergency provision of liquidity to financial markets when there is a systemic problem (e.g. in the 2008–2009 credit crisis).

In 2014, the Bank established a new mission to 'promote the good of the people of the United Kingdom by maintaining monetary and financial stability'. It aims to bring under its control responsibility for:

- microprudential supervision
- macroprudential policy
- monetary policy.

This means that the Bank should now be in a better overall place to deliver key economic benefits:

- stable inflation
- economic growth
- the continuous provision of financial services.

The MPC sets the interest rates it believes are needed to achieve the government's inflation target. At the moment the UK government has an inflation target of 2%.

Monetary Policy

The Bank's monetary policy objective is to achieve price stability (i.e. low inflation) in the economy and, subject to that, support the government's economic objectives, including those for growth and employment. Price stability is defined by the government's inflation target of 2%.

Price stability is regarded as important because:

- it helps businesses and consumers plan, which encourages spending and investment
- it helps the international price competitiveness of products.

Unanticipated inflation can:

- erode the real value of households' savings
- reduce the real value of employees' earnings (if the nominal pay is not keeping pace with inflation)
- increase costs, which reduces profits for investment
- make exports uncompetitive, which reduces aggregate demand in the economy.

The 1998 Bank of England Act made the Bank independent to set interest rates. This means that the interest rate is set to achieve the inflation target rather than to achieve political aims.

The Inflation Target

The UK government has an inflation target of 2% based on the **Consumer Prices Index (CPI)**.

If the target is missed by more than one percentage point on either side, the Governor of the Bank has to write an open letter to the Chancellor to explain why this has happened and what the Bank proposes to do to ensure inflation comes back to the target.

A target of 2% does not mean that inflation will actually be held at this rate constantly. This is because interest rates would be changing all the time, and by large amounts, which could cause unnecessary uncertainty and volatility in the economy.

The aim of the MPC is to set interest rates so that inflation is within its target range within a reasonable time period without creating too much instability in the economy.

How Does Monetary Policy Work?
The MPC changes its official interest rate (the bank rate) to keep the demand for goods and services and the supply of goods and services approximately in balance:

- If demand for goods and services in the economy exceeds supply, inflation will tend to increase.
- If supply exceeds demand, inflation tends to fall.

By changing the bank rate, the rate of interest that the Bank of England pays on reserve balances held by commercial banks and building societies, the Bank can influence many other borrowing and lending rates set by commercial banks and building societies. This will affect spending and prices increases:

- If inflation looks like it will be too high, the MPC will increase interest rates to dampen demand and push down prices.
- If inflation looks like it will be too low, the MPC will reduce interest rates to increase demand and pull up prices.

Increasing Interest Rates
Higher interest rates should:

- make saving more attractive and borrowing more expensive – this will reduce spending and aggregate demand, putting less upward pressure on prices and leading to lower inflation
- create more demand for the currency from abroad – this should lead to a lower exchange rate, which will reduce the price of imports and result in lower costs. It also increases the price of exports in foreign currencies, which will reduce demand for exports.

With higher interest rates, people may switch to saving and demand for assets falls. This:

- leads to lower asset prices (e.g. for land and gold)
- reduces peoples' wealth, which will reduce spending.

Lowering Interest Rates
Lower interest rates should:

- make saving less attractive and borrowing cheaper – this will increase spending and aggregate demand
- mean lower repayments on any borrowing for households and firms, which should increase disposable income or profit and also lead to more spending.

Lower interest rates also mean:

- investors will get a lower return in the UK than they could get elsewhere
- there will be less demand for pounds
- all others things remaining the same, the price of the pound will fall
- the fall in the pound will make exports relatively cheap
- export demand should increase due to the lower prices increasing aggregate demand.

(However, in reality, so many factors affect the exchange rate that changes in the interest do not have a predictable effect.)

If interest rates fall, there will also be more demand for assets, such as shares and houses, which will increase their price until the return on these assets has also fallen to similar levels.

Households and firms who now have higher valued assets are likely to spend more as they are wealthier.

Changes in interest rates affect spending, which leads to more demand and, therefore, will affect output and employment. They can also affect wage costs by increasing the demand for labour. This can have an impact on employees' expectations of inflation and influence the wages that they are prepared to settle on.

Interest Rate Changes and Time Lags

The maximum effect of a change in interest rates on output is estimated by the Bank of England to take around one year. The maximum impact on consumer price inflation usually takes up to about two years. This means decisions about interest rates are made based on what is expected to happen rather than what is happening at the current time.

There is no point increasing interest rates just because demand is high now. You should increase interest rates if you think demand is going to be too high in a couple of years' time. This highlights one of the problems of using interest rates to try and control the economy.

Quantitative Easing

If the Bank of England feels the interest rate is not having the desired effect or more intervention is required it can use **quantitative easing (QE)**.

For example, in 2009, interest rates were very low but demand was not growing at the desired rate. At this point, the Bank introduced QE to stimulate the economy.

Quantitative easing occurs when a central bank creates new money electronically to buy financial assets (e.g. government bonds) from investors (e.g. banks or pension funds). This increases the overall amount of funds in the financial system. By making more money available, the Bank of England hopes financial institutions will lend more to businesses and individuals, which will stimulate demand.

Buying assets and increasing their price reduces the interest rate on them, which should allow businesses to invest and consumers to spend more, resulting in an increase in demand in the economy. This process aims to directly increase private sector spending in the economy and boost demand to return inflation to its target.

Forward Guidance

Forward guidance involves the Bank of England outlining what is likely to happen in the future with interest rates.

The aim is to influence behaviour in the economy. For example, if the Bank makes it clear that it intends to keep interest rates low for the coming months, the high street banks are more likely to lend money to households and firms at low interest rates for longer periods of time. It provides more certainty in financial markets.

Funding for Lending Scheme

In 2012, the Bank of England and HM Treasury launched the **Funding for Lending Scheme (FLS)**.

This scheme is aimed at creating incentives for banks and building societies to boost their lending to the UK economy. It does this by providing funding to banks and building societies for an extended period, with both the price and quantity of funding provided linked to their lending performance.

The idea is that easier access to bank credit should boost consumption and investment by households and businesses. This increased demand should raise incomes and lead to faster economic growth.

Quantity Theory of Money

The **Quantity Theory of Money** states that the price level is proportionate to the money supply. This theory can be illustrated using the Fisher equation of exchange:

$MV = PT$

Where:

- M is the quantity of money
- V is the velocity of circulation, i.e. how often the money is used in a given period
- P is the average price level
- T is the output.

Example

If the money supply is £200 and the velocity is 2 times, then the total spending is £200 × 2 = £400

If output is 50 units, then the average price level must be £8:
£200 × 2 = £8 × 50

If the money supply increases to £400 and the velocity is still 2, then total spending is £800.

If output remains at 50 units, the price level will rise to £16:
£400 × 2 = £16 × 50

A doubling of the money supply has doubled the price level.

An increase in the money supply leads to inflation (i.e. the Quantity Theory of Money is seen to be appropriate) if V and T are constant.

This is why economists called monetarists want to control the growth of the money supply – they believe that excessive money supply growth is inflationary. However, this assumes that velocity and output stay constant.

If the economy is below capacity, an increase in money supply might lead to more spending and more output and not be inflationary.

SUMMARY

- The Bank of England is the UK's central bank. It is owned by the government but is responsible independently for monetary policy.

- The Monetary Policy Committee (MPC) sets the interest rates it believes are needed to achieve the government's inflation target.

- The MPC changes its official interest rate (the bank rate) to keep the demand for goods and services and the supply of goods and services approximately in balance.

- Quantitative easing (QE) occurs when a central bank creates new money electronically to buy financial assets from investors. This increases the overall amount of funds in the financial system.

- Forward guidance involves the central bank outlining what is likely to happen in the future with interest rates. The aim is to influence behaviour in the economy.

QUICK TEST

1. What is the role of Bank of England?

2. What is the role of the Monetary Policy Committee (MPC)?

3. What is the Funding for Lending Scheme (FLS)?

4. What is meant by 'quantitative easing'?

5. State **two** factors affected by a change in interest rates on the economy.

6. What is meant by 'forward guidance'?

7. Money supply is £10 million, velocity of circulation is 2 and the number of transactions is 5 million. What will the average level of prices be using the quantity theory of money?

   A   £2

   B   £4

   C   £8

   D   £50

PRACTICE QUESTIONS

1. Explain the roles of the Bank of England and Monetary Policy Committee (MPC).   [15 marks]
2. Evaluate the impact of lower interest rates on economic agents.   [25 marks]

Fiscal Policy and Supply-Side Policies

Fiscal Policy

Fiscal policy involves changes in the levels and nature of government spending and the taxation and benefit rates to influence the economy. Fiscal decisions are made by HM Treasury and announced in the budget statement.

An Increase in Government Spending
An increase in government spending on final goods and services (e.g. roads, defence or education) increases the injections into the economy and increases aggregate demand. This spending may be by central or at local government level.

A Decrease in Taxation Rates
If the government reduces the taxation rate, it increases the amount that can be spent on consumption out of each pound (it increases disposable income). This increases aggregate demand and the equilibrium income and output.

Forms of Public Sector Spending
There are different types of public sector spending:

- **capital expenditure** is spending on capital (long-term) projects, e.g. investing in the infrastructure of the country or building new schools
- **current expenditure** is spending on items used up in the given year, e.g. the salaries of NHS staff
- **transfer payments** are the transfer of money from one individual or group to another, e.g. welfare payments are transfer payments because they are not payments for final goods and services.

Public spending can help to:

- stimulate start-ups, entrepreneurs, investment and innovation (e.g. the government might subsidise or provide loans for start-ups), which in turn can stimulate productivity and economic growth
- improve living standards by stimulating the economy
- improve income equality by providing more benefits for low-income individuals.

However, spending needs financing, which can lead to higher rates of taxation and **crowding out**.

Crowding out occurs when the government has to increase interest rates to sell more debt. The higher interest rates attract lenders to lend to the government but discourage or 'crowd out' private sector investment.

Taxation

Taxes are charges placed by the government on consumers or firms. Taxes can be:

- **direct** – taken directly from income and profits such, e.g. income and corporation tax
- **indirect** – paid indirectly when buying something, e.g. VAT.

Taxes can affect:

- the incentive to work, e.g. high income tax may reduce the desire to work
- tax revenues, which can affect the budget position
- the incentive to invest in capital and innovation, which can affect the aggregate supply curve and growth in the economy
- income equality in the economy, e.g. tax rates on low and high-income earners can influence the Gini coefficient
- the price level, e.g. an increase in VAT can increase prices and increases in business rates can increase costs, which may be passed on to consumers in the form of higher prices
- imports, exports and the trade balance (by affecting costs and prices and through tariffs on imports)
- the likelihood that businesses will want to locate in a country and, therefore, the flow of **foreign direct investment (FDI)**.

The Laffer Curve
The **Laffer curve** shows the possible relationship between tax rates and tax revenue gained by the government:

- If the tax rate is 0%, the tax revenue is 0%.
- If the tax rate was 100%, no one would work or earn profits (as they would lose them all), so the revenue would be £0.

- As tax rates begin to increase from 0% the revenue will increase.
- At some point, increasing tax rates will become so high that the revenue will start to fall (as there is less incentive to work or generate profits).

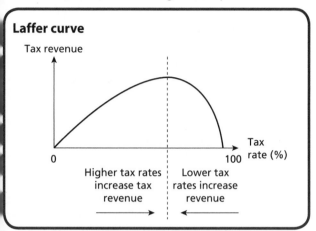

Laffer curve

Higher tax rates increase tax revenue | Lower tax rates increase revenue

Budget Deficits and Surpluses

The budget position shows the difference between total income and total spending by the government over a year.

If the total spending by the government over a year is greater than its receipts, the government will need to borrow to cover the difference. The gap between spending and receipts is known as a **budget deficit** or **public sector net borrowing**. This deficit will need to be financed, e.g. by selling government bonds.

If the total spending by the government over a year is less than its receipts, the government has a **budget surplus**.

Automatic or Cyclical Changes to the Budget Position

Changes in the budget position will automatically be affected by changes in the state of the economy. If national income increases, given existing policies and tax and benefits rates:
- more will be earned from taxes, such as income tax and corporation tax
- less will be paid on welfare benefits as more people are likely to be employed.

Automatically, the budget position will improve when the economy is in the growth phase of the economic cycle.

If national income falls, the budget position will automatically worsen.

The **structural deficit** is an estimate of how large the deficit would be if the economy was operating at a sustainable level of employment.

For example, if the economy was below its sustainable level, the actual deficit would be higher than the structural deficit. The difference is the **cyclical deficit**. It is caused simply by the state of the economy changing rather than any change in government policy.

The **headline deficit** figure is the difference between total receipts and total spending in a year.

The **current deficit** measures all receipts and current spending, but excludes spending on net investment, e.g. spending on long-term projects, such as building hospitals, investing in broadband or building a high-speed rail link. As long as the spending on net investment is positive, the current deficit will be smaller than the overall deficit.

Debt

A budget deficit or surplus occurs over a year. However, the government has been running deficits or surpluses (usually deficits) for many years. These add up to create the debt.

A **national debt** is the total amount of money owed at a given moment by a government. The deficit is a flow concept – it shows what has happened over a year in terms of inflows and outflows. Debt is a stock concept – it shows the financial position overall at a given moment in time.

- If a government has a budget deficit during a given year, this increases the national debt.
- If the government has a budget surplus in a given year, this reduces the national debt.

However, the debt can fall as a percentage of national income if the economy grows sufficiently. Also, some activities can increase the debt without being included in the deficit in any given year, including, most significantly, loans to students.

Problems of a Large Deficit or Large Debt
The government needs to fund its borrowing. This can lead to crowding out.

They may also involve an **opportunity cost** – spending on interest costs represents money that could be used for other investments.

High levels of debt may lead to a worse **credit rating** and make it more expensive to borrow in the future.

Reducing a Deficit
Reducing a deficit may involve:

- reducing government spending, e.g. through a reduction in services provided to the public
- increasing taxation revenue – this may involve new taxes or higher tax rates
- policies to promote long-term economic growth to bring about higher taxation revenue and less benefits spending.

Policies to reduce the deficit through spending cuts can involve an austerity programme, e.g. less spending in many government departments, which can reduce the services available and be politically unpopular.

The Office for Budget Responsibility (OBR)

The **Office for Budget Responsibility (OBR)** was created in 2010 to provide independent and authoritative analysis of the public finances of the UK.

The role of the OBR is to:

- produce economic and fiscal forecasts – it produces five-year forecasts for the economy and public finances twice a year
- assess performance against targets – this provides a judgement of the government's performance against its fiscal targets and its target for welfare spending
- assess the long-term sustainability of the public finances
- assess the fiscal risks of the forecasts.

Supply-Side Policies

Supply-side policies are government measures to increase the long-run aggregate supply in the economy. They are mainly microeconomic policies aimed at making markets work more efficiently.

A supply-side policy is a deliberate action by the government to bring about an improvement in supply side conditions.

The aim of supply-side policies is to:

- provide incentives to set up in business, innovate and be more productive

- develop entrepreneurial behaviour, e.g. start-ups and innovation
- develop technology to improve productivity
- encourage flexibility to enable people to move and accept jobs.

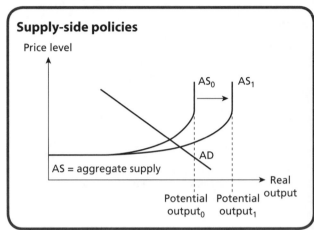

Supply-side policies

Supply-side policies aim to shift the long-run aggregate supply to the right and enable economic growth without inflation (providing the aggregate demand is also present).

Supply-side policies that increase the economic potential of the economy, shift the PPF outwards.

Market-Based Supply Side Policies
Market-based policies include:

- reducing government spending and borrowing
  - O less private sector funds are given to the government and instead can potentially be used more effectively by the private sector
  - O the government will not need to increase interest rates as much to raise funds and lower interest rates can stimulate private sector investment
- lower business taxes
  - O this can increase profits leading to more investment and research and development
  - O this can lead to new technology and more efficiency
- lower income taxes, which provide a greater incentive to work because employees retain more of each pound earned – this can increase the supply of labour
- reducing bureaucracy and regulations to make it easier for businesses to set up and operate

- changing employment laws to make it easier for people to be employed and accept jobs
- deregulating markets to allow more competition and make it easier for firms to enter
- improving incentives for people to look for work and accept jobs
- providing better information to help people find jobs
- increasing investment and research and development spending to improve productivity
- encouraging the start-up and expansion of new businesses and enterprises.

Interventionist Supply Side Policies

Interventionist policies involve direct intervention in the economy by the government. For example the government can:

- invest in key infrastructure projects (e.g. broadband and transport links) to make it easier to move products around the country and be more productive
- invest in a regional policy to help deprived areas and stimulate investment
- invest in an industrial policy to help specific industries, e.g. to protect infant or developing industries that need time to expand and gain economies of scale to be internationally competitive
- manage the exchange rate to keep its value relatively low to help exports become more competitive, e.g. use low interest rates to reduce demand from abroad for the currency or by selling the currency in return for foreign currencies.

The Effect of Supply-Side Policies

Supply-side policies shift the long-run aggregate supply outwards. This should lead to non-inflationary growth and more employment (whereas demand-side policies can lead to higher prices).

SUMMARY

- **Fiscal policy involves changes to government spending on final goods and services and tax and benefit rates to influence the economy.**
- **The budget position measures the difference between government income and spending over a year. It is a flow concept.**
- **The national debt shows total amounts owed by the government – it's a stock concept.**
- **Supply-side policies aim to shift the long-run aggregate supply outwards.**
- **Supply-side policies aim to make markets (e.g. the labour and goods markets) more efficient and more competitive.**

QUICK TEST

1. What is measured by the government's budget position?
2. What is meant by a 'budget surplus'?
3. What is meant by the 'structural deficit'?
4. What is meant by the 'current deficit'?
5. What is meant by a 'national debt'?
6. What is the relationship between the budget position and the debt position?
7. What is the difference between structural and cyclical deficits?

PRACTICE QUESTIONS

1. Explain the possible demand-side consequences of a decrease in taxation rate. **[15 marks]**

2. Evaluate the view that the present policy of the government to reduce its deficit through lower government spending is unnecessary. **[25 marks]**

Globalisation and Emerging Economies

Globalisation

Globalisation occurs when there is greater integration of economies, industries, societies and cultures around the world.

The Organisation for Economic Cooperation and Development defines globalisation as:
'The geographic dispersion of industrial and service activities, for example research and development, sourcing of inputs, production and distribution, and the cross-border networking of companies, for example through joint ventures and the sharing of assets.'

Globalisation has made the world more interdependent and means that economic change in one country will have effects on other economies around the world.

Effects of Globalisation
Greater globalisation has involved:

- greater movement of goods, services, people and money around the world, including more FDI
- the development of global brands, e.g. coffee shops (Starbucks), cigarettes (Marlboro), fast food (McDonalds), perfumes and fashion (Dior)
- outsourcing of products around the world and global supply chains.

Look at what you wear, eat, use to get around and communicate with. Where was it produced? The chances are that it was produced abroad or at least many of its components were.

Globalisation – Contributing Factors
The increase in the links between countries is due to:

- a fall in communication costs – it is easier than ever before to communicate via the phone or Internet, so it is easier to operate and manage businesses globally and overcome the potential diseconomies of scale that could be caused by being on separate sites
- better transportation links, e.g. faster, cheaper air travel – this makes it easier to move products around

- containerisation – shipping costs have fallen significantly since the introduction of containers, which make it easier, cheaper and more secure to ship large quantities around the world
- differences in tax systems – it is desirable for multinationals to operate in different countries to benefit from such differences
- fewer protectionist measures, such as tariffs and quotas, have made it easier to trade internationally.

Multinational Companies (MNCs)
Multinational companies (MNCs) are companies that have bases in more than one country. An international business may trade in several countries but a multinational has bases abroad.

Companies may become multinational:

- to access resources in different countries, e.g. they may want minerals from Region A, cheap labour in Region B and design capabilities in Region C – by operating multinationally they can make use of the best skills and resources in each area
- to spread risks by operating in different regions, e.g. if there was a strike in one country, other units could carry on operating
- to benefit from government incentives by locating in a particular region, e.g. tax incentives or grants
- to overcome trade barriers, e.g. by operating within a customs union rather than trying to sell into it. For example, if a business operates within the European Union and uses enough supplies from other European Union countries, it can export within the Union with no barriers to trade. If it was trying to export from outside the Union, it would face trade barriers, such as tariffs (taxes).

A government may welcome multinationals because they:

- can bring jobs – this can reduce unemployment and stimulate economic growth, helping the government to achieve its objectives

- can bring expertise and technology – this can help increase aggregate supply
- can bring investment – this can help increase aggregate supply.

However, multinationals may:

- exploit local resources and not invest the profits in the local area – the profits may be returned to the home country leaving a sense of exploitation
- use local labour only for low level jobs and leave the high level jobs (such as senior management) to employees from the home country
- not take into account the external social costs of their actions in terms of their impact on the local economy and environment.

Developing Economies

World Bank Income Classification (2013)

As of July 2013, the World Bank income classifications by **gross national income (GNI)** per capita are as follows:

- low income: $1025 or less
- lower middle income: $1026 to $4035
- upper middle income: $4036 to $12 475
- high income: $12 476 or more.

Low and middle income economies are sometimes referred to as **developing** or **emerging economies**. These include Afghanistan, Angola, Papua New Guinea, Rwanda and Sierra Leone.

Features of Developing Economies

Each developing country is different and so it can be dangerous to generalise. China, Bolivia and Eritrea may all be developing economies, but they are radically different in many ways, e.g. population size and growth rates. However, the features of a developing economy often include:

- relatively low income per person
- low levels of productivity
- high levels of natural resources
- a high dependence on primary product exports
- high levels of external debt
- large numbers of people living in agricultural areas
- fast population growth
- low literacy rates
- high infant mortality rate, death rate and birth rate, along with low life expectancy

- relatively young population
- poor infrastructure (e.g. poor telecommunications, transport and energy)
- political and economic instability
- corruption within the system.

Problems Facing Developing Economies
A Dependency on Primary Products

A dependency on primary products, such as crops, is a particular problem for many developing economies. The long-run trend of prices on primary products is often downwards. These products are income inelastic so, as economies grow, the growth in demand does not grow proportionately. At the same time, developments in technology (such as farming technology) will increase supply. This brings down the long-run equilibrium price. The fall is relatively high as demand for primary products is likely to be price inelastic.

Primary products are subject to price and income instability. Changes in the weather or diseases can lead to inward shifts in supply. Given that demand is price inelastic, there can be significant changes in price and also in producers' incomes.

Producers face monopsony power of large companies from developed economies who can push down prices. Changes in supply can lead to significant changes in price and producers' incomes.

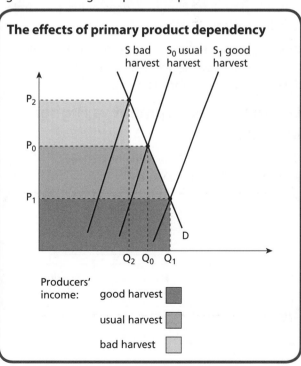

The effects of primary product dependency

Low Levels of Capital Accumulation

The governments of developing countries often have relatively few funds to invest in the development of human capital (e.g. through education and training):

● Domestic investment may be low due to instability, a lack of clear property rights and a poor financial system.
● Foreign Direct Investment (FDI) may be low due to the political and economic instability and corruption.

This lack of human and physical capital may limit the growth of the economy.

Inefficiency

As developing economies attempt to diversify into new markets, they have second-mover disadvantage. They do not have the scale of the producers from the more developed economies, so do not have the same economies of scale. This may mean they are uncompetitive.

Protectionism of the Developed Economies

There may be protectionist measures in place that prevent developing countries from gaining access to certain markets.

For example, the Common Agricultural Policy of the European Union protects European farmers and makes it difficult for farmers in developing economies to gain access to the market.

Corruption and Political and Economic Instability

Corruption and political and economic stability can deter FDI and internal investment.

Economic Development vs Higher Incomes

Michael Todaro stated the three objectives of economic development were:

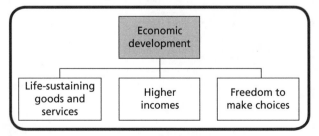

Life-Sustaining Goods and Services

The objective is to increase the availability and widen the distribution of life-sustaining goods and services, such as food, shelter, health and protection.

Higher Incomes

The objective is to improve the standard of living, including, in addition to higher incomes, more jobs, better education and greater attention to culture. This leads to greater individual and national self-esteem.

Freedom to Make Choices

The objective is to increase the range of economic and social choices available to individuals. To do this, they must be set free from servitude and dependence, not only in relation to other people and nation states, but also to the forces of ignorance and human misery.

Economist Amartya Sen argues that development provides an opportunity for people to free themselves from suffering caused by:

● early mortality
● persecution
● starvation / malnutrition
● illiteracy.

Therefore, economic development is about greater political, cultural and social freedom and not just about increasing incomes.

The most common measurement of development is the **Human Development Index (HDI)**, which is published each year by the United Nations Development Programme

The HDI was developed to highlight the view that people and their capabilities were a better measure of the development of a country than just economic growth.

The HDI is a summary measure of average achievement of a number of important dimensions, including health, education and standard of living:

● The health dimension is measured by life expectancy at birth.
● Education is measured by the mean years of schooling for adults aged 15 years and over and expected years of schooling for children entering education.
● The standard of living is measured by gross national income per capita.

Human Development Index (HDI)

Human development index (HDI)	Dimensions	Long and healthy life	Knowledge		A decent standard of living
	Indicators	Life expectancy at birth	Mean years of schooling	Expected years of schooling	GNI per capita (PPP $)
	Dimension index	Life expectancy index	Education index		GNI index

Human development index (HDI)

The HDI has a value from 0 to 1:

- 1 is totally developed.
- 0.8 and above is highly developed.
- 0.5 to 0.8 is medium developed.
- Under 0.5 is a low level of development.

PRACTICE QUESTION

1. Using examples to illustrate your answer, explain the difference between economic growth and economic development.   **[15 marks]**

Growth and Development

Strategies Influencing Growth and Development of an Economy

The growth of an economy will usually be measured by changes in **gross domestic product (GDP)**. This measures changes in national income.

Market-Orientated Approaches

Market-orientated approaches to promote growth in developing economies may involve:

- reducing barriers to trade – this allows:
  - cheaper imports, which can lead to greater efficiency
  - more exports, because a country can negotiate lower protectionism from it in return for lower barriers to trade against its producers
- encouraging FDI (e.g. through tax incentives or subsidies) – this can bring in investment, technology, expertise and new products and processes
- removing government subsidies to inefficient industries, which will force them to compete with producers globally
- encouraging **micro-finance** schemes (financial services made available to help entrepreneurs and start-ups) – this is a way of promoting economic development, employment and economic growth
- privatising industries – this puts more resources into private ownership and encourages competition and greater efficiency in pursuit of profits.

As the name suggests, market-orientated approaches open up markets to the forces of supply and demand. This puts pressure on businesses to be more efficient.

Interventionist Policies

Interventionist policies to stimulate growth in developing economies may involve:

- greater investment and development of human capital through training and better education
- greater investment in infrastructure projects (e.g. to improve communication and transports) – this can help promote business within the economy and help make trade easier and more efficient

- promoting joint ventures with global companies to benefit from their expertise and technology
- establishing government **buffer stock schemes** (e.g. buy when there is excess supply and sell where there is excess demand) to stabilise prices and help with planning
- investing to develop the tourist industry – this will help bring in spending from abroad and encourage investment.

Interventionist policies involve the government playing an active role in helping to create an environment that brings about more growth in the economy.

Foreign Direct Investment (FDI)

Foreign direct investment (FDI) refers to investment from one country to another. It involves setting up operations or acquiring the controlling assets, including shares in other businesses. Typically, control of another business is regarded as having 10% or more of its shares.

FDI may also involve transferring management, technology and organisational skills. It can bring new ways of doing business to a local firm and help to make it more competitive and give it access to new markets.

FDI may be:

- **horizontal** – this occurs when the company carries out the same activity as at home, e.g. Toyota producing cars in the UK as well as Japan
- **vertical** – this occurs when a different stage of the production process is added:
  - **forward vertical integration** is when the business moves closer to the final customer, e.g. a car manufacturer buys a car dealership
  - **backward vertical integration** is when the business moves back towards its suppliers, e.g. a car manufacturer buys a tyre manufacturer
- **a conglomerate** – this occurs when an unrelated business is acquired, e.g. a car manufacturer acquires a hotel business.

The Lewis Model of Economic Development

The **Lewis model** of economic development is based on a model of the economy with two sectors:

- rural agriculture
- urban manufacturing.

It is assumed that labour is mainly employed on the land. Labour is regarded as a variable factor of production and land as a fixed resource.

Lewis assumes that:

- initially, most labour in is the countryside and there is a surplus
- variable factors are added to the fixed factor in the agricultural sector
- at some point, there will be diminishing returns to a factor – there are not sufficient tasks for the additional worker to do, so there is a fall in its marginal product.

Meanwhile:

- urban workers are working in manufacturing in the cities
- they are producing a higher value added output and earning higher wages
- these higher earnings act as an incentive and attract the agricultural workers to migrate to the cities to join the manufacturing sector.

Manufacturing businesses are more productive because of technology. They generate higher profits. The profits are invested into more equipment, which further increases productivity.

This model may explain some of the urbanisation that occurs when economies are developing and growing. It explains how an economy transitions from being mainly agricultural to being more urbanised.

The shift from rural to urban is happening at the moment in many economies in Africa and also in China.

However, in reality:

- migrating workers may not be able to find or take a job in the cities due to lack of information or skills – labour may not be able to move easily from the countryside to the cities

- manufacturing firms may invest in technology that does not require high levels of labour.

Harrod-Domar Model of Economic Growth

The **Harrod-Domar model** of economic growth argues that savings and investment are key determinants of economic growth. It tries to explain why growth does not happen in some economies.

A **growth strategy** refers to the policies a government may use to promote more growth in the economy, e.g. supply-side policies.

The Harrod-Domar model states that the rate of growth in an economy depends on:

- the level of national saving (S)
- the capital-output ratio, e.g. if £40 of capital is required to produce an additional £10 per year of output, the capital output ratio is 4:1.

With a low capital output ratio, a relatively high level of output can be produced with a relatively low level of capital. If the quality of capital resources is high, the capital-output ratio should be high.

$$\text{Rate of growth in GDP} = \frac{\text{savings ratio (\%)}}{\text{capital–output ratio}}$$

Example
If the savings rate is 10% and capital-output is 5, the economy would grow at:

$$\frac{10\%}{5} = 2\% \text{ per year}$$

If the capital output ratio was 2, the growth rate would be:

$$\frac{10\%}{2} = 5\% \text{ per year}$$

Therefore, according to this model, increasing growth requires:

- more savings (as a % GDP)
- a lower capital-output ratio (as a result of better quality capital).

Developing economies often have low saving rates (because of low incomes) and a poor capital-output ratio (as capital is not especially productive).

Therefore, to improve the growth rate of a developing economy, savings need to be encouraged to fund investment. However this may not be easy. In many developing economies, the marginal propensity to consume (the extra spending out of each extra pound) is high and households may not be able to or want to save. This may not be helped by the lack of a reliable and trusted financial system.

It is also important to improve the quality of capital, e.g. by supporting the adoption of new technology. However, this may not be easy to achieve due to a lack of research and development.

The Importance of Trade

Trade can be an important part of the development of an economy because it can provide:

- an increase in aggregate demand through exports
- more jobs, which leads to multiplier effects within the economy
- a source of foreign exchange
- a source of finance to invest in technology and innovation.

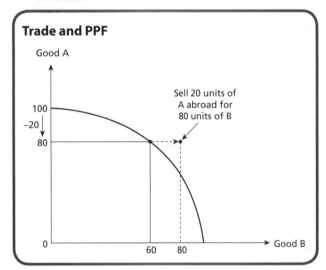

Trade and PPF

Good A

Sell 20 units of A abroad for 80 units of B

100
−20
80

0   60   80   Good B

A country may sacrifice 20 units of A. If resources were transferred into B, it would produce 60 B, but by selling its output abroad, it may trade for 80 units of B.

However, trade can cause problems for developing economies, e.g. the volatility of some global commodities means that price changes can have major effects on the exporting economy.

The Value of Aid in Promoting Economic Growth

Aid is seen by some as a way of promoting economic growth in developing economies.

Types of aid include:

- **bilateral aid** – aid from one country to another
- **multilateral aid** – aid allocated by a global organisation
- **project aid** – the direct financing of specific projects
- **humanitarian aid** – funds given in an emergency, e.g. for disaster relief or to help with a refugee crisis
- **debt relief** – this may take the form of cancellation, rescheduling, refinancing or reorganisation of a country's external debts.

Benefits of Aid

Aid can:

- enhance a country's **growth potential**, but the effects may not be seen for many years
- overcome the lack of savings in the economy to fund investment
- fund major infrastructure projects
- improve productivity by developing the human capital.

Disadvantages of Aid

Aid may:

- take time, e.g. aid to help improve education may take many years to have a real impact
- not be used effectively due to corruption
- may make an economy too dependent on aid
- distort market forces and lead to less efficiency as resources are diverted to the wrong sectors.

The UK government has a target of allocating 0.7% of GDP to overseas development assistance (ODA).

Debt Relief

Cancelling debt or reducing debt repayments of developing economies frees up funds for governments to use for productive investment. However:

- cancelling debt does not deal with the underlying problems, so debt may accumulate again over time
- it is important to ensure the additional funds are used productively.

Non-Government Organisations (NGOs)

A non-governmental organisation (NGO) is a non-profit, voluntary organisation that is independent from the government.

There are many types of NGOs. Some will promote policies to help developing economies. For example:

- they may provide information and advice on how aid can and should be used
- they may fund various projects themselves
- they may lobby government for change
- they may try to reduce monopsony power exerted by developed economies by raising awareness.

The World Bank defines NGOs as: 'Private organisations that pursue activities to relieve suffering, promote the interests of the poor, protect the environment, provide basic social services, or undertake community development.'

There are now thousands of NGOs working to support developing economies. Some may pursue a single policy objective, such as greater access to AIDS drugs in developing countries or press freedom. Others will pursue broader goals, such as eradicating poverty or greater human rights protection.

SUMMARY

- **Foreign Direct Investment (FDI) refers to investment from one country to another that involves setting up operations or acquiring the controlling assets, including shares in other businesses.**
- **A non-governmental organisation (NGO) is a non-profit, voluntary organisation.**
- **Debt reduction involves cancelling debt or reducing debt repayments.**
- **The Harrod-Domar model states that the rate of growth in an economy depends on the level of national saving (S) and the capital-output ratio.**
- **Stimulating growth in developing countries may involve market-orientated or interventionist policies.**

QUICK TEST

1. Outline the Harrod Domar model of growth.
2. State **two** types of aid given to developing countries.
3. Name the **two** sectors that are the focus of the Lewis model of growth.
4. What is an NGO?
5. Explain **one** reason for giving aid to a developing country.
6. What is meant by 'microfinance'?

PRACTICE QUESTION

1. Discuss the view that free trade is more effective than aid in promoting economic development in developing countries. **[25 marks]**

Trade

International trade occurs when one country sells and buys goods and services from another. It involves:

- sales abroad (exports)
- purchases from abroad (imports).

International trade occurs because one country can produce products at a lower **opportunity cost** than another, i.e. it has a **comparative advantage**.

A country can benefit from trade by growing faster than it could on its own. It is able to specialise in the production of some products where it has a comparative advantage and sell these abroad at a profit. This specialisation means it can benefit from internal economies of scale, which lead to even lower unit costs.

Trade also allows businesses to import items more cheaply than they can produce them themselves, leading to lower costs, more profits, more investment and growth.

International trade involves imports and exports, which allows a country to enjoy a wider range of goods and services at lower prices than it could produce on its own.

International trade allows a country to enjoy a wider range of goods and services at lower prices than it could produce on its own – it gives consumers more choice of products and businesses more choice of supplies.

Absolute advantage occurs when a country can produce products at a lower cost than a competitor. It is possible for a country to have an absolute advantage in many (even all) products. However, there will still be possibilities for trade, due to the differences in how much of one product has to be sacrificed for another unit of another product, i.e. because of differences in the opportunity cost and comparative advantage of different products.

Example

Resources in each of two economies are divided equally into the production of products X and Y.

	Product X	Product Y
Country A	4	4
Country B	1	2

Country A can produce more of both products. It has an absolute advantage in production.

However, if you consider the sacrifice required to produce one item of each:

	Product X	Product Y
Country A	1X = 1Y	1Y = 1X
Country B	1X = 2Y	$1Y = \frac{1}{2}X$

- Country B can produce fewer units of Y, but the opportunity cost is lower than in Country A.

The Benefits of Trade

Example
Resources in each of two economies are divided into the production of products X and Y.

	Product X	Product Y
Country A	1	4
Country B	2	3
Total	**3**	**7**

In terms of opportunity cost:

	Product X	Product Y
Country A	$1X = 4Y$	$1Y = \frac{1}{4}X$
Country B	$1X = \frac{3}{2}Y$	$1Y = \frac{2}{3}X$

- Country A has a comparative advantage in the production of Y because it has a lower opportunity cost.
- Country B has a comparative advantage in the production of X because it has a lower opportunity cost.

All resources are now diverted into the industry that has a lower opportunity cost. Each economy specialises. It is assumed that doubling the resources will double the output, i.e. there are constant returns to scale. This means:

	Product X	Product Y
Country A	0	8
Country B	4	0
Total	**4**	**8**

- By specialising resources where each country has a comparative advantage, the total world output has increased.

Given the differences in the opportunity cost, countries can trade and this can be mutually beneficial.

For example:

- Country B can sell 1X for more than $\frac{3}{2}Y$ – this more than covers its opportunity cost. It could sell for $\frac{3}{2}Y$, which would just cover its opportunity costs.
- Country A can buy 1X for less than 4Y – this would be cheaper than producing it itself. It could buy it for 4Y, which would cost the same as making it for itself.

The terms of trade (i.e. the amount of one product that could be traded for another) would therefore be in the range:

$$\frac{3}{2}Y < 1X < 4Y$$

For example, if 1X was sold by Country B for 2Y, it would make a profit for this country whilst still being cheaper for A than it would cost to make it itself.

The **Law of Comparative Advantage** states that countries should specialise in producing products where they have comparative advantage.

The benefits of trade may be even greater than those suggested if there are gains of specialising, e.g. if doubling resources in an industry more than doubles output (this is called increasing returns to scale).

A potential disadvantage of trade would be if the industries experienced decreasing returns to scale.

Production Possibility Frontier (PPF)

The benefits of trade can be shown using a **production possibility frontier (PPF)**.

A country can sell some of the output of the product where it has comparative advantage abroad (e.g. product X) for more of other products (e.g. product Y) than it could produce domestically. This means it can now consume outside of the PPF.

Trade and the PPF

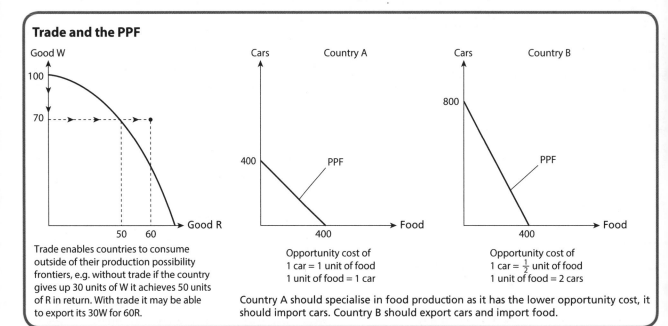

Trade enables countries to consume outside of their production possibility frontiers, e.g. without trade if the country gives up 30 units of W it achieves 50 units of R in return. With trade it may be able to export its 30W for 60R.

Opportunity cost of
1 car = 1 unit of food
1 unit of food = 1 car

Opportunity cost of
1 car = $\frac{1}{2}$ unit of food
1 unit of food = 2 cars

Country A should specialise in food production as it has the lower opportunity cost, it should import cars. Country B should export cars and import food.

SUMMARY

- Comparative advantage occurs when one country can produce a good or service with a lower opportunity cost than another.

- Free trade occurs when there are no barriers to trade between countries.

- Free trade removes tariffs and quotas between members. A single market removes other non-tariff barriers to trade.

- Trade enables countries to consume outside of their production possibility frontiers.

1. Which of these determines whether a country has a comparative advantage over a trading partner?

   A   its level of money wages

   B   imposing a higher level of tariffs

   C   greater productive capacity in some goods

   D   a lower opportunity cost in the production of some goods

2. Colombia and Zambia both produce copper and emeralds.

   The diagram shows the PPF for each country.

   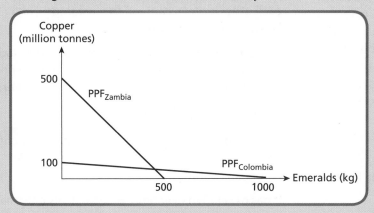

   Which of the following statements is correct?

   A   Colombia has an absolute advantage in the production of copper.

   B   Zambia has an absolute advantage in the production of copper.

   C   Zambia has an absolute advantage in the production of emeralds.

   D   Neither Zambia nor Colombia has an absolute advantage in the production of emeralds.

PRACTICE QUESTION

1. Examine why international trade has benefited UK consumers.   **[15 marks]**

Competing Abroad

International Competitiveness

The international competitiveness of an industry depends on whether it has a comparative advantage and how much the products sell for abroad.

This competitiveness abroad depends on:

- the productivity in the industry – the higher the better, as high productivity should lead to lower unit costs, lower prices and greater competitiveness
- unit costs, e.g. wages and land costs – the lower these are the more competitive an industry should be
- the exchange rate – if the pound is strong, it has a high value and is expensive in terms of other currencies, which will make a country's products less competitive, all other factors being equal
- the quality of the product and design – the better the quality of the products, the more competitive an industry is likely to be.

Barriers to trade are factors that limit trade between countries. These include:

- tariffs (taxes of imports)
- quotas (limits on the number of imports)
- government policies to buy domestic products or regulations that make it difficult or expensive for foreign goods to enter the domestic market (e.g. a great deal of paperwork and bureaucracy).

Free trade occurs when there are no barriers to trade, i.e. trade between countries is unrestricted. It can lead to:

- economic growth, by providing markets to sell exports to (boosting demand) and access to cheaper inputs
- a wider choice of better quality products for consumers and firms
- lower world prices due to greater competition.

Trading Blocs

Trading blocs are groups of countries that join together and have free trade between each other. For example, countries in the European Union have removed barriers to trade between each other but have common barriers to trade with non-members.

Other trading blocs include:

- NAFTA (North American Free Trade Area) between North America, Mexico and Canada
- Mercosur – a customs union between Brazil, Argentina, Uruguay, Paraguay and Venezuela
- ASEAN (Association of Southeast Asian Nations).

Trade within trading blocs, such as the European Union, has significantly increased.

Countries within a trading bloc tend to trade with each other more because of the free trade. This is known as **trade creation**.

However, this diverts trade away from previous trading partners (often because of barriers to trade with non-trading bloc members), which is called **trade diversion**.

European Union (EU)

The European Union (EU) is an economic and political partnership which, at the moment, involves 28 European countries.

It has developed over time to become a 'single market', allowing goods and people to move around, as if the member states were one country. It is easy to move goods around the Union.

The EU has:

- its own currency, the euro, which is used by 19 of the member countries
- its own parliament, which sets regulations in many different areas, e.g. transport and consumer rights.

The UK joined the EU in 1973. The EU has continued to grow in size. The biggest enlargement happened in 2004 when ten new member countries joined. Romania and Bulgaria joined in 2007 and Croatia was the latest to join in 2013.

Becoming a member of the EU is a complex procedure that requires countries to meet various criteria in their economies. Any country that satisfies the conditions for membership is allowed to apply. These conditions are known as the 'Copenhagen criteria'. They include:

- a free market economy
- a stable democracy and the rule of law
- the acceptance of EU legislation.

EU Budget

The three main sources of revenue for the EU are:

- a small percentage of the national income of each member country
- a small percentage of each member country's standardised value-added tax revenue
- a large share of import duties on non-EU products.

Currently the largest share of EU spending is on creating economic growth and jobs within member countries. It also aims to reduce economic gaps between countries.

Other areas of spending include:

- agriculture, rural development, fisheries and environmental protection
- combating terrorism, organised crime and illegal immigration.

Brexit

Brexit is the name given to the decision for the UK to exit from the European Union.

The UK population voted (by 52% to 48%) to leave in 2016 and the details are now being negotiated under Article 50.

The reasons for voting to leave were a mixture of political and economic. For example:

- some people wanted to stop the freedom of movement into the UK from other EU countries
- some wanted to stop paying into the EU budget fund
- some wanted the UK to be free to negotiate its own trade deals with countries outside of the EU.

The UK government must now negotiate the terms under which it trades with other EU members.

What happens to UK trade with former EU members following Brexit will depend on the terms of the Brexit deal. When it was in the EU, the UK had trade barriers with non-members. All EU members had the same barriers. Once it leaves the EU, the UK may be able to trade more easily with non-EU countries in Africa, Asia or the Middle East.

International Trade

Free Trade Area

A free trade area is one where there are no tariffs, taxes or quotas on goods and / or services from one country entering another.

The European Free Trade Association (EFTA) includes Norway, Iceland, Switzerland and Liechtenstein as members.

Single Markets

A **single market** eliminates barriers to trade, such as tariffs, quotas or taxes. It includes the free movement of goods, services, capital and people.

A single market also aims to remove so-called 'non-tariff barriers', such as different rules on packaging, safety and standards.

For example, in the EU there are regulations covering many industries and products within all countries that belong to the EU. These include food standards and health and safety. This attempts to create a level playing field between countries and does not happen in a free trade zone.

For goods, the single market in the EU was largely completed in 1992, but the market for services is an ongoing process.

Customs Union

A **customs union** occurs when countries join together and agree to apply the same tariffs to goods from outside the union.

Norway is part of the EU's single market, but it is not part of the customs union – it sets its own tariffs on goods imported from outside the single market. However, most Norwegian goods are imported tariff-free into the EU.

Other Options

Three members of EFTA are also almost full members of the single market: Liechtenstein, Iceland and Norway. They have negotiated access to the single market (excluding agriculture and fish). They have to implement EU single market rules and regulations in their own countries, but do not have any influence over what these policies are.

Switzerland has negotiated a series of bilateral deals that give it access to the single market for most industries, although it also has to apply EU rules and pay money to the EU.

The World Trade Organisation (WTO)

The World Trade Organisation (WTO) aims to:

- reduce barriers to trade around the world
- negotiate agreements between countries to enable freer trade
- help producers of goods and services, exporters, and importers trade more easily.

Protectionism

Protectionist measures are designed to protect one country's producers from foreign competition.

Protectionism can be used to:

- protect an infant industry, i.e. a new industry that needs time to grow and benefit from economies of scale and be competitive (protectionist measure may be removed later)
- retaliate against a country that has imposed protectionist measures
- serve as a political bargaining weapon, e.g. to change a government's policies regarding nuclear weapons
- protect a vital industry, e.g. the defence industry or farming.

Most of these reasons are political rather than economic.

Protectionism can be popular with a government because it is seen to act. Producers of a domestic industry that is struggling can be well organised and lobby for protectionist measures to limit foreign competition. This leads to higher prices and poorer quality for consumers, but consumers are usually badly organised and have little lobbying power, so are ignored.

Types of Protectionist Measures
Tariffs

Tariffs are taxes on foreign goods and services and increase their price. Consumers will switch to the relatively cheaper domestic products. The effect depends on the price elasticity of demand. The government earns revenue from the tax on imports.

Quotas

Quotas are limits on the quantities of goods and services that are allowed into a country. This restriction drives up prices and allows domestic producers to sell more.

Legislative Barriers

Differences in regulations, such as health and safety, can make it difficult or expensive for foreign producers to produce products that can gain access to a market.

Export Subsidies

If a government provides aid to domestic producers it will shift the domestic supply downwards by the subsidy. This is because costs have been reduced. This enables domestic producers to be more price competitive.

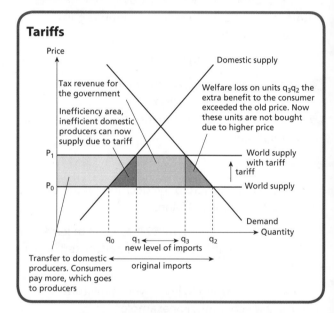

Tariffs

SUMMARY

- **Protectionism occurs when there are barriers to trade between countries.**
- **A customs union has free trade between members and common barriers of trade against non-member countries.**
- **The European Union is a customs union; Brexit occurred when the UK voted to leave this in 2016.**
- **There are various forms of protectionism such as tariffs and quotas.**

1. The diagram shows the demand and supply of a product in an economy open to international trade.

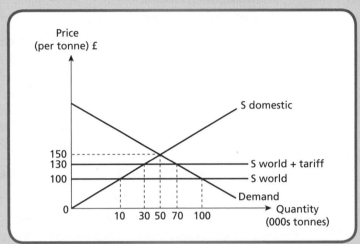

After a tariff is imposed, what is the total value of the revenue received by the producers?

A £3.9 million   B £9 million   C £5.2 million   D £9.1 million

2. The diagram shows the market for an internally traded product.

P^w = world price and P^{w+t} = world price, plus tariff.

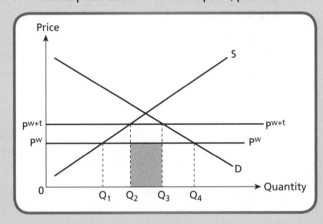

After a tariff is imposed, what does the shaded area represent?

A tariff revenue for the government   D the producer surplus for domestic producers

B revenue for domestic producers   E the welfare loss as a result of the tariff

C revenue for importers

PRACTICE QUESTION

1. Discuss the view that protectionist policies should be introduced to protect UK businesses.   **[25 marks]**

The Balance of Payments

The **balance of payments** is a record of all of a country's financial transactions with the rest of the world over a year.

The balance of payments account has three elements:

- the current account
- the capital account
- the financial account.

The balance of payments always balances as the supply and demand of pounds will always be equal, i.e. the number of pounds being changed into other currencies (supply of currency) equals the number being bought (demand). This means, for example, that a current account deficit must be matched by a surplus on the other areas of the balance of payments and vice versa.

The current account on the balance of payments includes the **balance of trade**, **income** and **international transfers**.

The Balance of Trade
The balance of trade measures the value of:

- exports, i.e. goods and services that are made by UK companies and sold abroad – they generate income for the country.
- imports, i.e. goods and services made abroad and sold to people in the UK – they represent money leaving the country.

The balance of trade can be divided even further by analysing the trade in goods (or visible trade) and trade in services (or invisible trade).

Income
Income refers to the income earned by UK citizens who own assets overseas. It includes:

- profits
- dividends on investments abroad (payments made to shareholders by companies who earn a profit)
- interest.

International Transfers
International transfers are usually:

- money transfers between central governments (who lend and borrow money from each other)
- grants, such as those that the UK has received as part of the Common Agricultural Policy from the European Union (EU). (Although the UK's transfers to the EU have usually been in deficit – the UK has given the EU more money than it has received.)

Factors Affecting the Current Account Position of a Country

Relative Inflation Rates and Exchange Rates
The current account position of a country will depend on relative inflation rates and exchange rates. These will affect the relative prices of a country's goods abroad and, therefore, how competitive it is.

For example, if a country has relatively high inflation rates, it will tend to make its products uncompetitive abroad, all other things unchanged, which will reduce export revenue.

If the value of a currency increases, exports become more expensive in foreign currencies overseas, which reduces sales and export revenue. This worsens the current account position.

Income Level
The income level of a country affects its spending on imports, so it also has an impact on its current account position.

The income of other countries will affect how much they are likely to buy, which will affect the country's exports.

If other countries that the UK trades with grow fast, it should increase demand for exports all other things being equal. If they are growing slowly, demand for exports may be lower.

Productivity
Increasing productivity in a country will reduce the unit costs of production and, assuming other factors are unchanged, this will make a country's goods and services more attractive abroad.

Current Account Deficit

If a country has a current account deficit, the value of money leaving the country on the current account is greater than the value of money entering the country.

If there is a current account surplus, the value of money entering the country on the current account is greater than the value of money leaving the country.

A current account deficit may mean:

- a country is importing a higher value of goods and services than it is exporting – this may improve living standards, because consumers are consuming more products
- a country is importing valuable capital equipment – this may improve its country's productive capacity in the long run and increase aggregate supply.

Therefore, in the short run, a current account deficit may not be a problem.

However, a deficit means that import spending is greater than export earnings, which reduces aggregate demand and can lead to higher rates of unemployment.

In the long run, a current account deficit:

- can reduce jobs in domestic industries because they are uncompetitive
- can reflect a long-term underlying lack of international competitiveness
- may lead to a fall in the value of the currency, which increases import prices and causes cost push inflation.

Reducing a Current Account Deficit

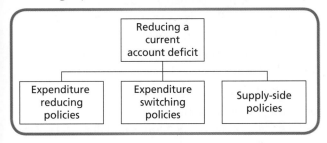

Expenditure Reducing Policies

Expenditure reducing policies aim to reduce total spending in an economy.

Reducing aggregate demand will reduce spending on imports. The extent of the fall in import spending will depend on:

- the amount that income falls
- the size of the marginal propensity to import.

However, reducing aggregate demand can lead to slower growth and unemployment in the country.

Expenditure Switching Policies

Expenditure switching policies aim to get consumers to switch to domestic products and away from foreign products. They include:

- tariffs (taxes on foreign products) and quotas (limits on the number of imported items), which:
  - lead to higher prices and less choice for consumers
  - allow inefficient domestic producers to produce (because they are protected)
  - may also lead to retaliation by other countries.
- reducing the value of the currency – this makes exports cheaper in foreign currency and imports more expensive, which help the competitiveness of the country.

Supply-Side Policies

Ultimately the current account deficit occurs because the country is uncompetitive.

Supply-side policies can increase completion, innovation, quality and service, helping the country to export more. They should help increase efficiency, reducing unit costs and enabling exporters to lower their prices. However, they may take time to take effect.

The J-Curve Effect

A **depreciation** of a currency occurs when its value falls in price.

A **devaluation** occurs when the government deliberately takes actions to reduce the currency's value. For example, the government may sell its currency in return for foreign currency.

The **J-curve effect** shows how, following a depreciation of the exchange rate, the current account position on the balance of payments may get worse before getting better.

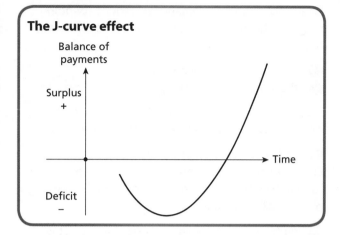

The J-curve effect

If a government reduces the value of its currency, it makes exports relatively cheap abroad and imports relatively expensive domestically.

A Rise in Export Sales

If export sales rise, a country will earn more export revenue. The effect of this will be greater in the long run, as more buyers switch to these lower price items from alternatives (it often takes time for consumers and business to switch from existing products to new cheaper ones). This means export revenue will rise to some extent in the short run but to a greater extent in the long run.

Demand for exports in the short run is probably not very sensitive to price changes, as customers are used to certain suppliers. Over time, customers find new, cheaper suppliers and so demand for exports becomes more price elastic.

The Effect of a Weak Currency

The effect of a weak currency is to increase the price of imports in the domestic currency.

In the short run:

- demand for imports is likely to be price inelastic because contracts will have been signed and consumers and businesses do not know where else to find supplies
- the percentage fall in the purchases of imports is less that the price increase
- total spending on imports increases and the current account position can worsen.

Over time, demand for imports becomes more price elastic. Over time, domestic businesses and households will switch away from the more expensive imports, which will reduce the spending on imports.

Therefore, the effect of a depreciation (fall in value) of the currency depends on the price elasticity of demand for exports and imports. The more responsive these are to price changes, the more the currency account position will improve.

According to the **Marshall Lerner condition**, the current account position will improve if:

price elasticity of demand for exports + the price elasticity of demand for imports > 1

In the very long run, the higher import prices from the depreciation or devaluation of the currency may lead to cost push inflation and make the country uncompetitive. This can lead to a worsening of the current account position again.

The International Monetary Fund (IMF)

The International Monetary Fund (IMF) is an organisation of 189 countries that work together to encourage:

- global monetary cooperation
- financial stability
- more international trade
- higher levels of employment
- sustainable economic growth
- less poverty.

Its main purpose is to ensure the stability of exchange rates and international payments.

Most resources for IMF loans are provided by member countries, primarily through their payment of quotas. The IMF reviews country policies and national, regional and global economic and financial developments through a formal system known as surveillance.

The IMF advises its 189 member countries, encouraging policies that foster economic stability, reduce vulnerability to economic and financial crises and raise living standards.

Quota Subscriptions

Each member country of the IMF is assigned a quota to contribute, based broadly on its relative position in the world economy.

Special Drawing Rights

Special drawing rights are an international reserve asset, created by the IMF in 1969, to supplement its member countries' official reserves.

Financial Assistance

IMF financing provides its members with breathing room to correct balance of payments problems. National authorities design adjustment programs in close cooperation with the IMF that are supported by IMF financing.

SUMMARY

- The balance of payments is a record of all of a country's financial transactions with the rest of the world over a year.

- A current account deficit means the value of money leaving the country on the current account is greater than value of money entering the country.

- The J-curve effect shows how a depreciation of the currency might worsen the current account of the balance of payments before improving it.

- The Marshall Lerner condition states that, if the value of the price elasticity of demand for exports plus the price elasticity of demand for imports is greater than 1, a depreciation of the currency will improve the current account.

QUICK TEST

1. What is the balance of payments?

2. What is meant by a 'current account deficit'?

3. What is the aim of an expenditure switching policy?

4. What is the aim of an expenditure reducing policy?

5. What is the J-curve effect?

6. What is the Marshall Lerner condition?

7. What is the role of the International Monetary Fund (IMF)?

8. What is the role of the IMF?

PRACTICE QUESTION

1. Is devaluing the currency the best way of reducing a current account deficit? **[25 marks]**

Glossary

Abnormal (or supernormal / supranormal) profit when total revenue is greater than total costs

Absolute advantage when a country can produce products at a lower cost than a competitor

Absolute poverty severe deprivation of basic human needs, including food, safe drinking water, sanitation facilities, health, shelter, education and information

Agent a decision-maker

Aggregate demand a measure of the total planned spending on final goods and services at different prices; the total demand in the economy; measured by the equation: $AD = C + I + G + (X - M)$

Aggregate supply a measure of the total planned output of final goods and services at each and every price, all other factors unchanged

Allocative efficiency when output matches demand; the combination of goods produced and consumed must be such that, if the combination is changed, one consumer cannot be made better off without another consumer being made worse off (in terms of consumer satisfaction)

Allocative inefficiency the price paid is greater than the cost

Altruism an unselfish concern for other people's welfare

Anchor a piece of information that acts as a reference point when decision-making and influences the choice made

Asymmetric information when one part of a market knows more than another

Availability bias the idea that individuals are influenced by events and information that are most easily remembered (most readily available) when decision-making

Average cost (AC) unit costs; total costs ÷ output

Average fixed cost (AFC) fixed costs ÷ output

Average product (average returns to a factor) total product (output) ÷ the number of variable factors

Average revenue (AR) a measure of the amount paid by customers per item; the price of a product

Average variable cost (AVC) variable costs ÷ output

Backward vertical integration one business joins with another at a stage nearer the source of the products, e.g. a manufacturer acquires a supplier

Balance of payments a record of a country's financial transactions with the rest of the world over a year

Balance of trade a measure of the value of exports and imports

Balance sheet a snapshot of a bank's financial position at a given moment in time

Bank deposits an example of broad money; an IOU from commercial banks to consumers

Barriers to trade factors that limit trade between countries

Base (or central bank) money IOUs from the central bank, including currency and central bank reserves

Behavioural economics introduces psychology to traditional economics to try and understand decision-making more effectively

Bilateral aid aid from one country to another

Bond market the market in which IOUs sold by companies and governments are traded

Bounded rationality the idea that employees have time constrains, do not have perfect information and have cognitive limitations, all of which affect their ability to make optimal decisions

Bounded (or limited) self-control the idea that individuals do not have absolute self-control, as illustrated by habits and addictions

Break-even point the point at which price just equals average cost

Broad money money consumers have available for transactions, made up of currency and bank deposits

Budget deficit government spending is greater than taxation revenue

Budget surplus government spending is less than its revenue

Buffer stock scheme an intervention method used by the government to stabilise prices in volatile markets by buying when there is excess supply and selling where there is excess demand

Capital financial and material wealth; goods used to produce other goods, e.g. equipment and technology

Capital expenditure spending on capital (long-term) projects, e.g. investing in infrastructure of a country

Capital market provides medium to long-term finance; made up of the primary market (bonds and shares sold for the first time) and secondary market (the trade in second-hand shares)

Cartel a group of firms join together to act like a monopolist

Central bank responsible for overseeing a country's monetary system, e.g. The Bank of England

Central bank reserves IOUs from the central bank to commercial banks

Choice architecture influencing the choices people make by designing different ways to present the choices to them

Classical economists (liberal economics) the traditional belief that markets function best with minimal government interference

Collusive behaviour when firms have an agreement to work together, especially with regard to price setting in a market

Commercial bank high street banks, such as Barclays, Lloyds, the Royal Bank of Scotland and HSBC

Community surplus (welfare) producer surplus plus consumer surplus

Comparative advantage when one country can produce a good or service at a lower opportunity cost than another

Competition and Markets Authority (CMA) an organisation responsible for promoting competition, both within and outside the UK, for the benefit of consumers

Competition policy government policy aimed at protecting consumers and businesses from abuse by dominant firms

Conglomerate when a firm acquires an unrelated business, e.g. a car manufacturer acquires a hotel business

Consumer Prices Index (CPI) measures changes in the price of consumer goods and services purchased by households

Consumer surplus the difference between the price consumers are willing/able to pay for an item (because of the utility it provides) and the price they actually pay

Contestable market a market where there are low barriers to entry and exit

Contribution the difference between revenue and variable costs; a sum of money given to help pay for something

Contributory benefit a benefit towards which individuals or employers make a contribution into the National Insurance Fund, e.g. state pension and jobseeker's allowance

Coupon the annual interest payment on a bond

Creative destruction the idea that the abnormal profits earned by a monopoly act as an incentive for others to be innovative (creative) to remove (destroy) it

Credit creation where banks make more loans to consumers and businesses, with the result that the amount of money in circulation increases

Credit risk the probability that an individual or firm will not be able to pay back a loan

Crowding out occurs when the government increases interest rates to sell more debt – the higher interest rates attract lenders but discourage or 'crowd out' private sector investment

Currency banknotes and coins, which are an IOU from the central bank

Current deficit a measure of all receipts and current public spending, excluding spending on net investment, e.g. long-term projects

Current expenditure refers to public spending on items used up over the year, e.g. NHS salaries

Customs union occurs when countries join together and agree to apply the same tariffs to goods from outside the union

Debt borrowed money that has to be repaid with interest

Debt relief this may take the form of cancellation, rescheduling, refinancing or reorganisation of a country's external debts

Demerger businesses that have joined together through takeovers and mergers decide to separate and become separate business again

Depreciation a fall in value

Devaluation occurs when the government deliberately takes actions to reduce the currency's value

Developing (or emerging) economy a low or middle income economy; characterised by relatively low income per capita, low levels of productivity, high levels of natural resources and a high dependence on primary product exports

Direct tax a tax taken directly from earnings, e.g. income tax and corporation tax

Discrimination to treat an individual or group of people less fairly

Dynamic efficiency changes in efficiency over time

Equality the state of being equal

Equity refers to fairness (in relation to taxation, etc.); shares

Equity market the market in which shares are traded

Export subsidy help given to exporters by the government, e.g. a cash subsidy or a rebate

External growth when a business grows by joining with another (integration)

Fiat currency banknotes and coins that are not convertible into another asset, such as gold

Financial Conduct Authority (FCA) regulates the conduct of 56 000 financial services firms and the financial markets in the UK

Financial intermediaries organisations that provide a link between savers and borrowers, e.g. banks, pension funds and insurance companies

Financial markets markets that allow funds to move from those with excess funds (more than they wish to spend) to those lacking funds (wish to spend more than their income), including the money markets, capital market and foreign exchange market

Financial Policy Committee (FPC) the body responsible for monitoring the economy of the UK

Financial Services Act an act passed in 2012 that implemented the current regulatory framework for the financial system and financial services in the UK

Fiscal policy the means by which a government adjusts its spending levels and tax rates to monitor and influence a nation's economy

Fixed costs (FC) costs that do not change with output e.g. rent

Foreign exchange market is the market in which different currencies are bought and sold

Forward guidance when the central bank outlines what is likely to happen to interest rates in the future

Forward market setting a price at which to buy and sell currency at some point in the future; used by exporters and importers to protect themselves against possible movements in the exchange rate

Forward vertical integration when a business joins with another at a stage nearer the customer, e.g. a manufacturer buys a retailer

Frame the way that a choice is described and presented to individuals

Free trade when there are no barriers to trade

Funding for Lending Scheme (FLS) a scheme designed to incentivise banks and building societies to boost their lending in the UK real economy

Game theory the idea that firms must anticipate how competitors will act and react to different situations and take this into account when decision-making

Geographical immobility employees cannot move to or work in another region, e.g. due to prohibitive housing prices / transport costs

Gini coefficient a measure of the degree of income or wealth inequality in an economy; the higher the coefficient, the greater the degree of inequality

Globalisation integration of economies, industries, societies and cultures around the world

Gold standard a monetary system in which the currency has a value linked to gold (it is agreed that paper money can be converted into a fixed amount of gold)

Gross domestic product (GDP) a measure of the income earned in an economy over a year, i.e. the value of the output of final goods and services produced in a year

Gross national income (GNI) gross domestic product plus incomes earned by foreign residents, minus income earned in the domestic economy by non-residents

Growth strategy a policy that a government may use to promote more growth in the economy

Harrod-Domar model a model that tries to explain why growth does not happen in some economies; it argues that savings and investment are key determinants of economic growth

Headline deficit the difference between total receipts and total sending in a year

Heuristics mental shortcuts used in decision-making that allow you to make quick decisions

Horizontal equity when individuals in the same financial position are taxed in the same way

Horizontal integration when one business joins with another at the same stage of the same process, e.g. one bank joins with another bank

Human Development Index (HDI) a measure of economic development and social welfare, based on life expectancy, education and standard of living

Humanitarian aid funds given in an emergency, e.g. for disaster relief or to help with a refugee crisis

Income how much is earned over a given period; a flow of earnings

Income equality a measure of how income is distributed within an economy

Indirect tax a charge on products that is payable by producers to the government; it may be a specific per unit tax or an ad valorem tax

Indivisible describes an input that cannot be scaled down to produce a small quantity of output or a commodity that has a minimum size or quantity, below which it is not available

Inflation when there is a sustained increase in the general price level over a period of time

Innovation the introduction of new products and processes; the successful development of an invention

Interdependent when firms or economies depend on each other

Interest rate the cost of borrowing money (and the reward for saving)

Internal diseconomies of scale occur when the scale of production increases and causes costs to rise

Internal economies of scale occur when the scale of production increases and causes the average cost to fall

International Monetary Fund (IMF) an organisation in 189 countries, which works to foster global monetary cooperation, secure financial stability, sustainable economic growth and facilitate international trade

International trade when countries buy and sell goods and services from each other

International transfer a money transfer or grant between central governments

Investment bank a bank that specialises in helping companies with their finances

J-curve effect a J-shaped curve that shows how, following a depreciation of the exchange rate, the current account position on the balance of payments may get worse before getting better

Keynesians a group of economists who believe that the move from the short-run aggregate supply to the long-run aggregate supply is slow

Kinked demand curve model a non-collusive model that assumes firms compete against each other

Labour the human input into production; refers to the size and skills of the workforce

Laffer curve a curve showing the possible relationship between tax rates and tax revenue gained by the government

Law of Comparative Advantage countries should specialise in producing products where they have comparative advantage

Law of Diminishing Marginal Utility at some point, additional units of consumption lead to less extra satisfaction (utility)

Law of Diminishing Returns in the short run, as successive units of a variable factor are added to a fixed factor of production, the marginal product (marginal returns) of the variable factor will eventually fall

Legislative barrier a difference in regulations that makes it difficult or expensive for foreign producers to gain access to a market; a protectionist measure

Lewis model a model of economic development that looks at movement of labour: rural agriculture to urban manufacturing

Liabilities debts; money from different sources that must be repaid in the short term or long term

Liquid available funds

Liquidity risk occurs if there is a danger that a large number of depositors and investors may withdraw their funds at once, leaving the bank short of funds

Long run all factors of production are variable

Long-run average cost (LRAC) the minimum cost per unit with all factors variable

Lorenz curve the line of actual income distribution

Loss total revenue is less than total costs

Macroeconomics concerned with the economy as a whole

Macroprudential regulation regulation concerned with identifying, monitoring and removing risks that affect the stability of the financial system as a whole

Marginal condition profit maximisation occurs when marginal revenue equals marginal cost

Marginal cost (MC) the extra cost of producing a unit; change in total cost ÷ change in output

Marginal product (marginal returns) the change in output resulting from one more unit of a particular input, e.g. labour

Marginal revenue (MR) the revenue earned by the sale of an extra unit; change in total revenue ÷ change in output

Marginal revenue product the value of the extra output of the extra unit of labour

Marginal utility the extra satisfaction gained from consuming an additional unit of the product

Market made up of supply and demand; occurs when buyers and sellers come together to trade (exchange goods and services)

Market capitalisation the total value of a company's shares; share price multiplied by number of shares

Market liberalisation the deregulation of a market

Market share a company's sales as high percentage of the total sales in the industry

Market structure describes the number and size of the producers in the market

Marshall Lerner condition a theory that the current account position on the balance of payments will improve if the price elasticity of demand for exports plus the price elasticity of demand for imports is greater than 1

Merger when two or more businesses join together to create a new business

Microeconomics concerned with specific markets within an economy

Microfinance financial services made available to help entrepreneurs and start-ups

Microprudential regulation regulation that focuses on ensuring the stability of individual banks and other financial institutions

Minimum efficient scale (MES) the first level of output at which the long-run average costs are minimised

Monetary policy involves the central bank taking action to influence interest rates, the supply of money and the exchange rate to affect the economy

Monetary Policy Committee (MPC) a committee of the Bank of England, which decides the official interest rate in the UK

Money (nominal) wages the actual wages paid (opposed to real wages)

Money market provides short-term finance to firms and the government; involves trading in short-term debt, interbank lending and short-term government borrowing

Monopolistic competition a market in which there is the potential to make abnormal profits in the short run only

Monopoly occurs when there is a single seller in a market

Monopoly power occurs when one business dominates the industry and has power over others

Monopsony occurs when there is a single buyer of goods, services or labour in a market

Moral hazard occurs when people have an incentive to behave badly

Multilateral aid aid allocated by a global organisation

Multinational company (MNC) a company that has bases in more than one country

***n* firm concentration ratio** the market share of the top n firms in an industry

National debt the total amount owed by a government

National Living Wage (NLW) an estimate of how much people need to earn to cover the basic cost of living; a minimum legal level in the UK for wages for those aged 25 and over

National Minimum Wage (NMW) a minimum legal level for wages in the UK for those under the age of 25

Nationalisation when assets are transferred from the private sector to the public sector

Natural monopoly a type of monopoly that exists as a result of the high fixed costs or start-up costs of operating a business in a particular industry

Negative output gap when the actual output is below the potential output

Net migration the difference between the number of people coming into a country and the number leaving a country over a given period

Non-accelerating inflation rate of unemployment (NAIRU) an estimate of the level of unemployment at which the labour market is in equilibrium with no pressure on inflation to change

Non-contributory benefit benefits which do not require a contribution to have been made by the individual, e.g. housing benefit, carer's benefit and child support

Non-price competition when firms compete in areas other than price, e.g. through branding and advertising

Normal profit when total costs equal total revenue

Nudge a low-cost and simple technique used to change an individual's behaviour without reducing the number of choices available

Occupational immobility employees cannot move from one industry to another due to a skills gap

Office for Budget Responsibility (OBR) an office tasked with providing independent economic forecasts and analysis of public finances

Oligopoly when a few firms dominate an industry

Opportunity cost the alternative that is given up / sacrificed when a decision is made about resource allocation, e.g. if resources are allocated to produce more computer games they cannot also be used for healthcare

Organic (or internal) growth when a business grows by selling more of its products

Output gap the difference between the actual level of national output and the estimated potential level

Overall poverty a lack of income and resources to ensure that citizens have sustainable livelihood, characterised by hunger, ill health, limited access to education, unsatisfactory housing and social discrimination

Perfect competition when there are many firms in the industry, products are homogeneous (not differentiated), there is freedom of movement of businesses in and out of the industry in the long run and customers have perfect information

Phillips curve a curve showing a potential trade-off between inflation and unemployment

Policy the actions taken by governments in the economic field, including taxation, budget setting and controlling interest rates

Poll tax a tax which is a fixed sum of money per person

Positive output gap when the actual economy is above the potential

Price discrimination when a producer charges different prices for the same product

Price elastic a percentage change in price leads to a more than proportionate change in another factor

Price inelastic a percentage change in price leads to a less than proportionate change (less than 1) in another factor

Price maker a firm that sets the price in a market

Price taker a firm that can sell all of its output at the same price

Primary market when bonds and shares are sold for the first time

Principal refers to a business owner or shareholder who has an agent (manager) to act and make decisions on their behalf

Privatisation when assets are transferred from the public sector to the private sector

Producer surplus a measure of the difference between the price producers are willing and able to supply units at and the price they actually receive

Production possibility frontier (PPF) shows the maximum combination of goods and services that an economy can produce with its factors of production at a given moment

Productive inefficiency when an economy is operating inside the PPF, i.e. more of one product can be produced without producing less of another (resources are available)

Profit maximisation when a business earns the higher possible profit achievable

Project aid the direct financing of specific projects

Protectionist measures barriers to trade; measures to protect a country's producers from foreign competition

Prudential Regulation Authority (PRA) responsible for the regulation and supervision of around 1700 banks, building societies, credit unions, insurers and major investment firms

Public ownership when the government has control of an organisation

Public sector net borrowing a budget deficit; the gap between spending and receipts in public finances

Public sector net debt used as a measure of the UK national debt; gross total debt minus the assets that government could turn into cash if required

Quantitative easing (QE) when a central bank creates new money electronically to buy financial assets from investors and increases the overall amount of funds in the financial system

Quantity Theory of Money the theory that price level is proportionate to money supply, illustrated using the Fisher equation of exchange: $MV = PT$

Quota a limit placed on the quantity of a good or service allowed into a country

Real wages money (nominal) wages adjusted for inflation

Regulatory capture when a regulating body comes to identify with the problems of an industry and starts to work in their interests (rather than the interests of society as a whole)

Relative poverty when individual or household income falls below the national average or median income

Reserve ratio the amount that banks must hold back in reserve from deposits

Retrenchment when businesses get smaller, e.g. though demerger

Returns to a factor occur in the short run as a variable factor is added to fixed factors

Returns to scale occur in the long run as the scale of production is changed with more of all factors

Secondary market the trade of second-hand shares

Shadow banking system the financial intermediaries involved in facilitating the creation of credit across the global financial system but whose members are not subject to regulatory oversight

Shareholder an individual or firm that owns at least one share in another company

Short run at least one factor of production is fixed

Short-run average cost (SRAC) the minimum cost per unit for any level of output given a certain level of fixed factors

Shutdown point the point at which the price just equals the average variable cost

Single European Market (SEM) refers to the EU as one territory without any internal borders or barriers to trade

Single market a market that promotes the free movement of goods, services, financial capital and labour between a group of countries

Social marginal benefit (SMB) the net social value of a good or service

Social marginal cost (SMC) the net social cost of a good or service

Social norm a belief held by society or a group about how you should behave in a particular situation

Spot market involves the immediate changing of currency, i.e. the exchange rate if you change currency today

Static efficiency when there is the most efficient combination of resources at a given moment in time

Status quo bias to continue with a choice even after the decision has lost some or all of its benefit

Statutory monopoly when a monopoly is created by the government and is protected by law

Structural deficit an estimate of how large the deficit would be if the economy was operating at a sustainable level of employment

Sunk cost a cost that a business is already committed to and cannot be recovered

Supply-side policy government attempts to increase productivity and shift aggregate supply to the right

Systemic risk a risk that could lead to the collapse of the whole, or a significant part, of the financial system

Takeover (or acquisition) when one business gains control of another, e.g. by buying the majority of its shares

Tariff taxes on foreign goods and services that increase their price

Third degree price discrimination when a producer charges different prices for the same product

Total cost (TC) fixed costs plus variable costs

Total product (or output) the total amount produced by a business in a period

Total revenue (TR) the total expenditure by consumers; the total income of a business

Total utility the total satisfaction received from consumption

Trade creation when free trade encourages countries to trade with each other more

Trade diversion when free trade diverts trade away from previous trading partners

Trade union an organisation that represents employees and works to protect their rights

Trading bloc countries that join together in a group and have free trade between each other

Transfer payments the transfer of money from one individual or group to another

Utility consumer satisfaction

Variable costs (VC) costs that change with output, e.g. the costs of materials

Vertical equity when people in different financial circumstances are taxed differently

Vertical integration when one business acquires another at a different stage of the same process

Wage differential when wage levels differ between different labour markets

Wage elasticity of demand a measure of the sensitivity of demand for labour relative to wage changes, all other factors unchanged; measured by the equation:

wage elasticity of demand

$$= \frac{\text{change in quantity of labour demanded (\%)}}{\text{change in wages (\%)}}$$

Wealth the total of how much an individual or organisation owns; it is a stock concept as it takes stock of what they own

World Trade Organisation (WTO) an organisation that deals with the global rules of trade between countries

X-inefficiency occurs when there is little incentive for a firm to control its costs

Yield the annual interest payment, or coupon, on a bond given as a percentage of the market price of the bond

Exam Advice

- Make sure you know what each paper involves and what time you have available. If there are optional questions, make sure you know how many you need to answer.
- Read the question. The most common mistake students make is to answer a different version of the set question. Sometimes this is a major misinterpretation (e.g. writing about the causes of a change not the consequences). Sometimes the answer loses focus on the question, e.g. it argues why cutting taxes is a good way of increasing aggregate demand, not why it is the best way.
- Plan your answer. The best responses usually show evidence of planning. Think about the question and the possible arguments and then select the relevant ones. From the very start of the answer, make it clear what your point is. For extended response questions that are worth a lot of marks, the introduction of your answer should outline what the answer is – this is then supported in detail by the rest of the response.
- Write clearly. Make sure the examiners can actually read your answers.
- Do not cross things out. You cannot gain any marks for information that has been crossed out. There is no negative marking, so even if what you have written is wrong, it does no harm to leave it in. You may gain the odd mark for something within in.
- Use diagrams. Diagrams can support an argument very effectively. However, make sure they are drawn clearly and labelled accurately.
- Read the command word carefully and look at the number of marks. An analysis question needs a chain of reasoning. Think about the point you are trying to make and what the end point of your argument needs to be. Is it the effect on consumers or on government? If it is an evaluative question, is there balance in your response? Have you put forward competing arguments and weighed these up against each other. Is there a judgement and conclusion?
- Use the context. Make sure it is not just a theoretical answer. You will usually have some data or information in a case study and you need to make your response relevant to the given economic situation.
- Make sure your judgements are built on the arguments you have made. Your conclusion must be clearly linked to the points you have made. This again shows the benefit of planning.

The Assessment Objectives

You will be assessed at the end of your A Level Economics course by exam. All exam boards must assess the same skills (Assessment Objectives) in approximately the same proportions.
The Assessment Objectives are:

AO1

You need to be able to:
demonstrate knowledge of terms / concepts and theories / models to show an understanding of the behaviour of economic agents and how they are affected by and respond to economic issues
This objective is assessed by questions that ask you to 'define' or 'identify'.

AO2

You need to be able to:
apply knowledge and understanding to various economic contexts to show how economic agents are affected by and respond to economic issues.
This objective is assessed by questions that ask you to 'calculate', interpret trends or use your knowledge in a given situation.

AO3

You need to be able to:
analyse issues within economics, showing an understanding of their impact on economic agents.
This objective is assessed when you are asked to 'examine' or to 'analyse'. It requires a logical chain of reasoning.

AO4

You need to be able to:
evaluate economic arguments and use qualitative and quantitative evidence to support informed judgements relating to economic issues.
This objective is assessed when you are asked to 'assess', 'discuss' or 'evaluate'. You need to balance competing arguments.

Types of Question and Command Words

There are three types of question that will come up in your exam:
- multiple choice
- short written answer
- extended response.

These may be based on given data (data response questions) or require you to recall and use your knowledge of the subject.

The marks awarded for each question type vary slightly depending on the exam board. However, the requirements will be the same.

Multiple choice questions are worth one mark. Make sure you follow instructions and indicate your choice of answer clearly.

For questions that require short written answers, you will normally be given between two to six lines to write your answer on. The marks available for the question (1 to 4 marks, depending on exam board) will give you an idea of how many points / how much detail the examiner is looking for.

Remember to pay attention to command words:
Define – give a clear, concise meaning
Calculate – use the data provided and the appropriate equation to work out the value; remember to use the correct units
Draw / show / illustrate – produce a diagram or clarify using examples
Identify – name or describe the characteristics of something
Explain – give purposes or reasons
Analyse / examine – provide a logical chain of reasoning

Extended Response Questions

Extended response questions are an important part of your economics exam. They are used to assess the depth of your understanding and carry a lot of marks (anything from 8 to 25 marks, depending on exam board).
Any question featuring one of the following commands requires evaluation (AO4):
- **Discuss**
- **Assess**
- **Evaluate**
- **To what extent…**

You need to consider the different arguments or viewpoints. Analyse each point in turn, using examples and evidence, and consider its strength. To conclude your answer, you must be able to weigh up the different points against each other and make an informed judgement.

To gain full marks, your answer must:

- be well organised and structured in a logical way
- be well written with good use of grammar so that your meaning is clear
- use economic terms accurately
- show a good understanding of economic concepts, principles and models
- apply the relevant economic ideas to the given context
- use relevant and focused examples
- use data to support your response where appropriate
- recognise different viewpoints
- include well-focused critical analysis with clear, logical chains of reasoning
- include evaluative comments supported by relevant reasoning throughout the response and a final conclusion.

Marking Your Answers

For each practice question in this book, to help you mark your own answers, the key points that should be included in an effective answer are listed.

However, it is important to remember that you will only be awarded good marks in the exam if these points are communicated in a clear, accurate and well–developed way and your response meets all the criteria listed above.

Answers

Day 1

Page 4 Individual Economic Decision-Making

QUICK TEST

1. The extra satisfaction (for a consumer) from consuming an additional unit
2. The total satisfaction (for a consumer) from consuming a product
3. Total utility increases at a decreasing rate
4. Considers the psychological factors that influence decision-making
5. Describing and presenting a choice to individuals in a particular way (to influence the outcome)
6. A low cost, simple technique used to change an individual's behaviour without reducing the number of choices available
7. An imbalance of information / when one of the parties in a transaction has more information than the other
8. People face constraints in decision-making, so they cannot solve problems optimally and take short cuts to enable decision-making to be easier and quicker
9. B

PRACTICE QUESTIONS

1. To answer this question effectively you should:
   - explain what is meant by rational buying behaviour and what it assumes
   - explain two or three factors that may lead to buying behaviour not being rational, with examples, e.g. anchoring (the previous price paid ('was') for a product acts as an anchor and affects how a consumer views the current price ('now')) and loss aversion (e.g. people save in low return investments to avoid risk; people may be reluctant to sell shares if the price has fallen even if they could then use the money to earn much higher returns elsewhere).

   Remember, the key is to explain a few factors in depth rather than have several undeveloped points.

2. To answer this question effectively you should:
   - outline the traditional theory and behavioural theory of consumer choice
   - outline two or three possible policies the government might adopt, such as increasing the price via indirect taxes, advertising, policies to reduce a lack of information, e.g. more labelling, nudge techniques or social norming
   - consider factors that might affect the success of such policies, e.g. how price elastic demand is or the extent to which having more information is likely to affect behaviour
   - make an overall judgement on the relative success of alternative policies, considering the factors that might determine success.

3. a) To answer this question effectively you should:
   - explain the difference between social and private costs and benefits
   - state that, in a free market, individuals will make decisions based on private costs and benefits
   - explain that because the social costs of car travel are greater than the private costs, this will lead to over consumption, i.e. the pollution, congestion and longer travel times for others will not be considered in the free market
   - explain that the negative social effects of rail travel are likely to be lower than for cars, but the full social benefits of train travel may not be appreciated leading to under-consumption.

   Remember, using diagrams can help support your argument.

b) To answer this question effectively you should:
- analyse the effect of increasing the price of petrol
- show the effect of higher petrol prices on demand for car usage (remember, petrol is a complement of car usage – you could consider how strongly related the two are, i.e. what is the cross price elasticity?)
- outline other ways that car usage may be reduced, e.g. behavioural techniques to influence demand
- compare the different ways of reducing car usage (e.g. the success of different methods may depend on the extent to which the demand for cars is linked to the price of petrol)
- make an overall judgement, e.g. it may depend on the cross price elasticity of demand for car usage relative to the price of petrol vs the sensitivity of car demand to behavioural techniques, such as a nudge.

Page 8 Returns to a Factor and Returns to Scale
QUICK TEST
1. **a)** W
   b) Y
   c) If marginal returns are above average, the average is pulled up; if marginal returns are below average, the average falls
2. 4th employee / 150 units output
3. At least one factor of production is fixed
4. Increasing but at a slower rate
5. Total product is maximised
6. $(12 \times 5 =)$ 60 units
7. **a)** True
   b) Average costs will fall
8. In the short run, at least one factor of production is fixed; in the long run, all factors are variable

PRACTICE QUESTIONS
1. To answer this question effectively you should:
   - explain the meaning of the short run in economics
   - outline the Law of Diminishing Returns to a factor and why it occurs
   - explain the possible impact of this law, e.g. If each extra unit produces less, more of the factor will be required for each additional output. All other factors constant (such as wages), this will increase the labour costs of producing.
2. To answer this question effectively you should:
   - explain the meaning of the long run in economics
   - explain why, in the long run, the firm is interested in returns to scale rather than returns to a factor
   - describe the effects of increasing, constant and decreasing returns to scale
   - explain how returns to scale affect unit costs.

Page 12 Costs
QUICK TEST
1. The average fixed cost is the fixed costs divided by the output (number of units)
2. The output gap is the difference between actual output and potential output – the maximum level of output that could be achieved while maintaining stable inflation over a given time horizon. It depends on how many people are available to work and how many hours they are willing to put in (labour); the number of buildings, machines and computers that are available to work with (capital); and the efficiency with which they can be combined (productivity).
3. Total costs = $25 \times 40 = £1000$
4. Average fixed cost = $£30 – £25 = £5$; fixed costs = $40 \times £5 = £200$

5. Because fixed costs are spread over more units.
6. If the extra cost is positive and increasing, total cost increases at an increasing rate.
7. Total costs do not change; there is no extra cost.
8. Variable costs = total costs – fixed costs = £20 000 – £12 000 = £8000
   Average variable cost = $\frac{VC}{Q} = \frac{£8000}{400} = £2$
9. Output = $\frac{£400}{£5} = 80$ units
10. At any moment, the business is in the short term with a fixed factor of production. As output increases, average costs change on the short run average cost. Over time, the fixed factor can be changed and the business moves on to a new short run average cost curve.
11. If the marginal (extra) cost is above the average, it pulls the average up. If the marginal is below the average, it pulls the average down. This means the marginal costs cross the average cost as the minimum point of the average cost.

PRACTICE QUESTION
1. To answer this question effectively you should:
   - outline the Law of Diminishing Returns
   - explain why the Law of Diminishing Returns relates to the short run (at least on fixed factor)
   - outline the meaning of internal economies of scale
   - explain how internal economies of scale are linked to changing the scale of production and long-run changes.

Page 16 Economies and Diseconomies of Scale
QUICK TEST
1. Purchasing economies of scale – as a business gets bigger and buys more, it will be able to negotiate lower prices from suppliers.
2. Communication diseconomies – as a business gets bigger, there are more people, more divisions and departments. Communicating becomes more difficult and can be slower and less effective, leading to bad decisions and higher unit costs due to inefficiency.
3. These occur when the unit costs are lower at every level of output due to changes outside of the business.
4. First level of output at which average costs are minimised.
5. False
6. False, unit costs fall.
7. False, unit costs fall at every level of output.
8. True

PRACTICE QUESTIONS
1. To answer this question effectively you should:
   - explain the meaning of the minimum efficient scale (MES)
   - explain what is meant by market structure
   - explain the importance of the possible cost disadvantages of not operating at the MES, e.g. The cost disadvantage of not operating at the MES depends on the existence of internal economies of scale. The greater the economies of scale, the greater the cost disadvantage of not being at the MES.
   - consider the importance of the MES in relation to demand in the market and analyse the importance of the cost disadvantage of not producing at MES, e.g. A high MES and high cost disadvantage means there will be relatively few businesses in the industry. This is because inefficient businesses could not compete because of the cost disadvantages. The efficient firms would easily undercut the inefficient firms and force them to close.

- make a judgement on the importance of the MES, e.g. Its influence on the structure of a market depends on the MES relative to overall demand in the market and the extent to which unit costs are higher at lower levels of output.

2. To answer this question effectively you should:
    - explain what is meant by unit costs (average costs)
    - explain why unit costs may increase as scale increases, i.e. diseconomies of scale
    - explain how a business might benefit from internal economies of scale
    - discuss whether internal diseconomies of scale are inevitable and consider whether there are actions businesses can take to avoid them, e.g. Some firms create separate businesses as they grow and run each one individually to avoid diseconomies of scale. Businesses might focus on staff welfare to avoid demotivation and make them feel part of the business. The business might invest in IT to improve communications.

Page 20 Revenues and Profits
QUICK TEST
1. C
2. C
3. C
4. Minimum point; if marginal is below the average, the average falls; if marginal is above the average, it pulls the average up
5. Occurs when total revenue equals total costs
6. Average fixed costs fall as output increases
7.

Price change	Price elasticity of demand	Effect on revenue
price increase	price inelastic demand	**revenue increases**
price increase	price elastic demand	revenue decreases

PRACTICE QUESTIONS
1. To answer this question effectively you should:
    - give the meaning of marginal, average and total revenue
    - explain why the marginal revenue may be equal to average revenue (if all units are sold at the same price) and why it may be below and diverge from average revenue (if demand is downward sloping)
    - explain that if marginal revenue is below average revenue this will bring the average revenue down
    - explain that marginal revenue shows the change in total revenue, e.g. if marginal revenue is positive, total revenue increases.

    Using a diagram might be an effective way of illustrating the points above.

2. To answer this question effectively you should:
    - explain what is meant by a loss (total revenue is less than total costs)
    - explain why firms cannot survive in the long run if they are making a loss
    - explain how in the short run businesses may be better off producing even if they make a loss, provided the revenue at least covers the variable costs, because a contribution is made to the fixed costs
    - conclude that a loss-making business might carry on producing in the short run if variable costs are covered by revenue.

Day 2
Page 24 Perfect Competition
QUICK TEST
1. Any two from: many firms; identical product; freedom of movement into and out of the industry; perfect information
2. A business can sell all of its output at the same price
3. Revenue is greater than costs
4. True
5. False
6. True
7. B
8. True
9. True
10. True

PRACTICE QUESTIONS
1. To answer this question effectively you should:
    - state what is meant by normal profits and abnormal profits
    - explain how abnormal profits will attract firms into the industry, e.g. Abnormal profits act as a signal to producers in other industries to come in and benefit from the high returns
    - explain how entry into the industry will shift the industry supply curve to the right and bring down the price – with more entrants, more is being produced at each price and the industry supply shifts outwards
    - explain how entry will stop when normal profits are made – at this point there is no further incentive to enter.

2. To answer this question effectively you should:
    - outline the features of perfect competition
    - explain how perfect competition is productively and allocatively efficient in the long run (price is equal to marginal costs and production is at the minimum of the average costs curve)
    - discuss the fact that firms in other types of market can make abnormal profit which may be used to finance research and development
    - discuss how the conditions for perfect competition are unlikely to exist and that market failures and imperfections exist, e.g. monopoly power and external costs and benefits – in this situation perfect competition may not be ideal, e.g. may actually lead to overproduction if there are negative production externalities.

Page 28 Monopoly and Monopsony
QUICK TEST
1. A single seller
2. Any two from: cost barriers; legal barriers; brand loyalty
3. True
4. True
5. False
6. The difference between the price producers are paid for a unit and the price they are willing to supply it at
7. True
8. True

PRACTICE QUESTIONS
1. To answer this question effectively you should:
    - state what is meant by abnormal profits
    - explain why abnormal profits encourage entry into the industry – they act as a signal to other firms to enter the industry to gain some of these high profits

- explain what barriers to entry are and why they enable a monopoly to make abnormal profits in the long run, e.g. government legislation, cost advantages, control of supplies, etc.

2. **a)** To answer this question effectively you should:
   - describe different forms of barriers to entry, e.g. legal, control of supplies, marketing, etc
   - explain how barriers to entry relate to monopoly but not to perfect competition and monopolistic competition
   - give real life examples of barriers, e.g. legal restrictions on delivery of letters / cost barriers for businesses wanting to enter the telecommunications industry / a few businesses have control over diamond distribution.

   b) To answer this question effectively you should:
   - outline what a monopoly is
   - outline why a monopoly may not be desirable, e.g. explain productive and allocative inefficiency, impact on prices, impact on consumer choice, concerns over quality, potential x-inefficiency
   - outline why monopoly may have some benefits, e.g. investment in research and development / dynamic efficiency / offsetting market failures, such as negative production externalities, by reducing output / may encourage others to innovate to gain abnormal profits
   - discuss government attitudes to monopoly, e.g. may intervene to regulate monopolies to protect customers / may be concerned about the abuse of monopoly power / may encourage monopolies, via patents, to reward and encourage entrepreneurs / may run its own monopolies to serve the public interest
   - make a judgement about the extent to which monopoly markets should be encouraged by governments.

Page 32 Other Market Structures

QUICK TEST
1. Firms work together
2. Prices are unlikely to change because an increase or decrease in price reduces revenue
3. Charging the highest possible price without encouraging entry to the market
4. Any two from: branding; product differentiation; loyalty cards / schemes; additional services
5. False
6. B
7. Firm A: monopolistic competition; Firm B: monopoly
8. True – it is assumed that a price increase is not followed by other firms; it is assumed a price decrease is followed.
9. True – firms work together as a monopoly.
10. False – it has a few relatively large firms.
11. False – they are independent.

PRACTICE QUESTIONS
1. Your answer should:
   - explain what is meant by an oligopoly
   - explain the importance of interdependence and how this can lead to competition and collusion
   - explain how collusion can lead to the same overall price and quantity as a monopoly
   - outline the problems of cartels and therefore a cartel is often unstable and may not end up with the price and output of monopoly
   - outline other models such as the kinked demand curve where firms do not collude
   - conclude that oligopoly can lead to the same price and output but it depends how firms behave towards each other.

2. Your answer should:
   - explain what is meant by an oligopoly
   - explain the importance of interdependence and how this can lead to competition and collusion
   - explain how price wars can reduce profits and are dangerous as a firm may be forced out of business
   - add that by keeping prices high (either through an explicit or implicit agreement), profit margins can be kept high – in this situation firms may compete through no price competition such as advertising
   - explain that the kinked demand curve model highlights why prices may be 'sticky'; if a firm increases price, this may not be followed and revenue may fall due to demand being price elastic; if a firm cuts its price, this may be followed meaning revenue may decrease due to demand being price elastic
   - conclude that this means that non-price competition is likely in oligopoly but price wars can exist.

Page 36 Monopolistic Competition and Price Discrimination

QUICK TEST
1. True
2. Any two from: age; time; gender; distance
3. False
4. False – there is no difference in costs; price discrimination occurs when there are differences in demand conditions.
5. False – consumer surplus will be zero.
6. True – if marginal revenue is higher in one market than another, the business would sell more there.

PRACTICE QUESTIONS
1. To answer this question effectively you should:
   - explain that different prices can be charged for the same product if markets are separated by preventing the transfer of goods and services, e.g. by time, age, gender, distance and barriers to entry, and that these markets may have different price elasticity of demand
   - explain that imperfect information may allow firms to charge different prices for the same product because buyers in one market may not know what others are paying
   - explain how producers will produce where the combined marginal revenue equals the marginal costs to profit maximise, i.e. they will produce where the marginal revenue is the same in each market (so there is no incentive to sell more in one of the markets), and that firms will charge a higher price in the more price inelastic demand
   - state that firms must be price makers and that it must not be possible to buy in the cheaper market and sell in the more expensive market.

2. To answer this question effectively you should:
   - define price discrimination
   - explain how price discriminators charge different prices for the same product in different markets – a higher price is charged when demand is price inelastic
   - show the effect on consumer and producer surplus of price discrimination
   - show how, e.g. with perfect price discrimination, consumer surplus is reduced and producer surplus is increased
   - show how by price discriminating, it may be possible to make a profit on some products that could not otherwise be produced as they would be loss making, i.e. can cross subsidise

- make a judgement on the statement that price discrimination only benefits producers, e.g. This is partly a question of perspective. Price discrimination does not just benefit producers, because some consumers get a product they would not otherwise get. However, others are charged more than they might be in a single price monopolist.

It might be useful to include a diagram to show how price discrimination may lead to some products being produced that would not otherwise be produced as they would be loss making.

3. To answer this question effectively you should:
   - define monopolistic competition and abnormal profits
   - explain how a profit-maximising monopolistic competitor sets price and output
   - explain how a monopolistically competitive firm can make abnormal profits in the short run
   - state that monopolistic competition does not have barriers to entry
   - explain how abnormal profits attract other firms into the industry and that this shifts demand inwards for any individual firm until normal profits are made – at this point there is no further incentive for other firms to enter because the rewards do not act as an incentive.
   - conclude that abnormal profits can be made in the short run but not in the long run because of freedom of entry and exit.

Day 3

Page 40 Business Objectives

QUICK TEST

1. The output at which marginal revenue = marginal cost
2. The output at which marginal revenue = 0
3. The highest output at which average revenue = average cost
4. Occurs when a decision or compromise is made to satisfice different interest groups
5. $\left(\frac{£20\,000}{£50\,000}\right) \times 100 = 40\%$
6. A
7. One business joins with another business in the same production process at a stage near the customer
8. One business joins with another business in a different production process
9. Any two from: value of sales; number of employees; number of outlets; value of assets; value of shares
10. The owners are shareholders and are different from the managers who control the business

PRACTICE QUESTIONS

1. To answer this question effectively you should:
   - define internal (organic) growth
   - compare internal growth with external forms of growth, i.e. mergers and takeovers – differences include the potential speed of growth; the difference between selling more and acquiring another business; external growth may lead to clashes due to differences in the way business is done, the culture and values of the business.

2. To answer this question effectively you should:
   - define horizontal integration (businesses join at the same stage of same production process)
   - explain the potential benefits of horizontal integration, e.g. internal economies of scale
   - consider the disadvantages of horizontal integration, e.g. may lead to internal diseconomies of scale if a business becomes too big
   - explain vertical integration and the difference between backward and forward vertical integration
   - outline the potential benefits of vertical integration, e.g. control of supplies (backward) or access to markets (forward)
   - consider the relative benefits and disadvantages of vertical and horizontal integration. These may depend on the objectives and circumstances, e.g. horizontal integration can lead to more market share and monopoly power, which could lead to higher prices and lower quality for consumers, whilst backward vertical integration may offset the monopoly power of suppliers.

Page 44 Competition, Technology and Efficiency

QUICK TEST

1. Businesses become more efficient over time
2. Invention creates a new idea; innovation takes the idea and ensures it is successfully launched
3. A
4. A market where there are low barriers to entry and exit, so new suppliers are able to enter the market and compete
5. B
6. Costs that a business is already committed to and cannot be recovered; if sunk costs are high, firms will compete aggressively to stay in the industry
7. Firms innovate to remove the established monopoly
8. The application of scientific knowledge for practical purposes, especially in industry
9. Any two from: new production methods, e.g. mass customisation; development of new products / markets; improve efficiency; reduce cost; affect competitiveness; destroy markets
10. Any two from : lower prices; more consumer choice; better quality; better service; innovation

PRACTICE QUESTIONS

1. To answer this question effectively you should:
   - define contestability
   - explain the impact of contestability on consumers, e.g. in relation to price, quality and service
   - explain the effects of greater competition and how this can improve the customer experience, e.g. Customers may experience a wider range of products, at lower prices and better quality and service.

2. To answer this question effectively you should:
   - define productive and allocative efficiency
   - explain what is meant by a monopoly market
   - explain how a lack of competition creates monopoly power
   - explain how a profit-maximising monopoly leads to allocative inefficiency (price greater than marginal cost) and productive inefficiency (not producing at the minimum of the average cost).

3. To answer this question effectively you should:
   - explain what is meant by efficiency and the different forms of efficiency e.g. allocative, productive and dynamic
   - outline the differences between competitive and monopoly markets, e.g. whether the firm is a price taker or a price maker, how many firms there are and whether there is freedom of entry and exit
   - explain how perfect competition leads to productive and allocative efficiency in the long run and show this on a diagram
   - compare perfectly competitive outcome with monopoly outcome in terms of efficiency using a diagram

- consider dynamic efficiency and the likelihood of this in perfect competition and monopoly
- consider how monopoly may correct market failures and therefore, in a second-best world, may be more efficient than perfect competition.

Page 48 The Labour Market
QUICK TEST
1. The demand for the final product directly affects the demand for labour
2. The value of the output of the extra employee
3. Changes in the wage rate
4. Greater productivity; an increase in demand for the final product
5. Any two from: a bigger labour force; immigration; less incentive to be unemployed (e.g. lower benefits)
6. Higher equilibrium wage
7. Lower equilibrium wage

PRACTICE QUESTIONS
1. To answer this question effectively you should:
   - explain how the wage rate brings about equilibrium in the labour market
   - show equilibrium using a supply and demand of labour diagram
   - explain why demand for labour may increase, e.g. due to greater productivity or an increase in demand for the final product
   - explain that an increase in demand leads to excess demand in the labour market and describe how the wage rate will increase to bring about equilibrium
   - explain how the extent of an increase will partly depend on how much demand increases and illustrate this idea using a diagram.

2. To answer this question effectively you should:
   - explain that the wage brings about equilibrium in the labour market
   - explain that the wage is likely to be higher if demand for labour is high – an increase in the demand for labour pulls up wages
   - consider why demand for labour might be high, e.g. employees are more productive or there is an increase in demand for the final product
   - explain that the wage may also increase when the supply of labour is limited, e.g. because high levels of skills are required to undertake a job
   - state that, in theory, employees would move from the low wage markets into high wage markets but this does not always happen due to barriers to entry
   - illustrate different demand and supply conditions in different labour markets leading to wage differences using examples, e.g. football players vs cleaners or chief executives vs administrative staff.

Page 52 Wage Differentials
QUICK TEST
1. The differences in wages that exist in different labour markets
2. Employees do not have the skills required to move into a different labour market
3. Employees cannot easily move to different area for a job, e.g. due to the costs of living and house prices
4. Employees must be paid at least this wage
5. There will be an excess quantity of labour supplied
6. It may restrict supply and increase wages

7. Employees are discriminated against, e.g. due to gender or ethnic origin – this is illegal
8. Hours of work (e.g. shift work, evening work); working conditions

PRACTICE QUESTIONS
1. To answer this question effectively you should:
   - explain what is meant by the National Minimum Wage
   - explain the possible effect on the quantity supplied and quantity demanded of labour of imposing a NMW above the equilibrium wage rate and show this on a diagram
   - explain how the effect depends on the level it is set at relative to the equilibrium wage, the impact on productivity (will output increase if employees feel more recognised and respected? will businesses focus on improving productivity through better working methods?) and on the wage elasticity of supply and demand for labour.

2. To answer this question effectively you should:
   - explain how wages are determined by market forces (i.e. explain how wages adjust to equate supply and demand of labour)
   - explain how and why wage differentials may occur and continue
   - explain how and why market forces may not work effectively, e.g. occupational and geographical immobility, trade union power, lack of information
   - explain that market forces do not explain wages in some sectors, e.g. public sector
   - use diagrams to support your arguments.

Day 4
Page 56 Income, Poverty and Wealth
QUICK TEST
1. Flow of earnings over a given period
2. The stock of assets a person, business or economy has at a given moment
3. When an individual or household's income falls below the national average or median income
4. A severe deprivation of basic human needs, including food, safe drinking water, sanitation facilities, health, shelter, education and information
5. Any two from: a loss of status and income; a decline in self-respect; health issues; sense of social exclusion, which can lead to social conflict
6. Any two from: unemployment; low pay; homelessness; addiction
7. Any two from: minimum wage; creation of jobs; a progressive tax and benefits system (accept any specific named policy, e.g. Tax Credits)
8. C
9. A

PRACTICE QUESTIONS
1. To answer this question effectively you should:
   - explain what is meant by income and income inequality
   - explain why income inequality can occur, e.g. due to the effect of unemployment, the nature of the tax and benefit system (e.g. some regressive elements), the high pay for some groups relative to others.

2. To answer this question effectively you should:
   - define income inequality
   - outline a number of policies that could be used to reduce income inequality, e.g. changes to the tax and benefit system, National Minimum Wage, efforts to create jobs

- evaluate the case for and against each of these policies, considering factors such as the likely cost, the length of time to take effect (this will interest a government, because it will want to be re-elected) and the potential consequences, e.g. higher tax on high income earners may affect the incentive to work.

Remember, it is better to deal with a few policies in depth than describe lots. It is the quality of the arguments that matter more that the number.

3. To answer this question effectively you should:
   - explain what is meant by the free market
   - explain how market forces determine earnings and allocate resources
   - explain how market forces may be efficient but lead to income inequality, e.g. different earnings between markets and wage differentials
   - show with diagrams how earnings might vary considerably due to different supply and demand conditions and labour immobility
   - explain how efforts to achieve greater income equality require government intervention, e.g. changes to tax and benefit system, minimum wage, policies to reduce unemployment
   - make a judgement that market forces in a free market lead to income inequality due to different market conditions, e.g. differences in labour supply and demand in labour markets. If equality is an aim then this requires government intervention.

Page 60 Public and Private Ownership

QUICK TEST
1. Transfer of assets from private sector to public sector
2. Transfer of assets from public sector to private sector
3. Any two from: to achieve social objectives; to remedy a market failure; to protect a strategic industry / 'way of life'
4. Any two from: x-inefficiency; productive inefficiency; lack of incentive; high prices / poor quality services for consumers; moral hazard
5. Any two from: raise revenue; create more shareholders; provide more of a profit incentive
6. The regulators start to represent the interests of those they should be regulating
7. Removing barriers to competition
8. Direct provision; regulation; tax or subsidy
9. Deregulation; competition policy; promoting start-ups
10. When a business dominates a market, e.g. has market share of over 25%

PRACTICE QUESTIONS
1. To answer this question effectively you should:
   - explain what nationalisation is
   - explain market failures and imperfections and inequality as reasons for governments to intervene and nationalise, e.g. to prevent overproduction if there are negative production externalities, to plan longer term as short-term investors may focus on short-term private rewards not long-term social benefits
   - explain why the government may nationalise for social motives, e.g. to prevent high prices of essentials such as energy and water that are regressive, to maintain jobs in some areas and sectors, to maintain earnings (potentially higher than market rates).

2. To answer this question effectively you should:
   - outline what privatisation is and its different forms
   - outline the reasons for privatisations, e.g. efficiency, the profit motive, to create shareholders
   - analyse the benefits and drawbacks of privatisation, e.g. in terms of competition and potential monopolies
   - consider the impact on different groups, e.g. consumers, government, producers and employees

- recognise that impact may vary, e.g. a privatised business may be more efficient and reduce prices for consumers but also cut jobs
- make a judgement about the extent to which privatisation is economically undesirable, e.g. it may depend on how and whether privatised industry is regulated, how the new owners behave and the extent to which private and social objectives differ.

Page 64 Macroeconomic Policy Objectives

QUICK TEST
1. Any two from: economic growth; low unemployment; stable prices; healthy balance of payments
2. More demand might reduce unemployment but increase prices
3. Output is above potential; high levels of demand pull up prices

PRACTICE QUESTIONS
1. To answer this question effectively you should:
   - define unemployment
   - explain how unemployment leads to a loss of output and is a waste of resources; the economy is likely to be below its potential output and inside the production possibility frontier
   - explain the impact of unemployment on tax revenue, welfare spending and the budget deficit
   - explain how unemployment can lead to inequality
   - explain how unemployment can have personal and social costs and low unemployment is good for the economy and also good for votes

2. To answer this question effectively you should:
   - define unemployment
   - identify other objectives of government
   - explain why reducing unemployment might be the objective of government
   - explain why other objectives might also be significant
   - consider why unemployment might be more or less important, e.g. how high is unemployment? What type is it? How high are the costs? What is the position of the economy relative to other objectives?

Page 66 The Phillips Curve

QUICK TEST
1. Non-accelerating inflation rate of unemployment
2. There is a trade-off
3. No trade-off
4. This means the economy is operating below its potential. This means demand may be low and there will be downward (deflationary) pressure on prices.
5. D

PRACTICE QUESTIONS
1. To answer this question effectively you should:
   - explain the meaning of NAIRU
   - analyse how a government might use expansionist policies to reduce unemployment below NAIRU
   - explain how real wages might fall using expectation augmented Phillips curve diagrams to illustrate this; reflationary policies may include increasing government spending on final goods and services or cutting taxation rates
   - analyse how the labour market might return to long-run equilibrium; adjustments in nominal wages will lead to changes in the real wage and bring it back to NAIRU level
   - discuss the views regarding how long it takes for the economy to return to the long-run equilibrium, e.g. The Keynesian view is that nominal wages are sticky and the economy is slow to return to the long-run equilibrium. Businesses cannot just

leave the market because the long run could be too long and as Keynes said, 'In the long run, we are all dead.' Classical economists would argue the labour market clears relatively fast and, therefore, it is very difficult for the government to keep unemployment below NAIRU for any length of time. Reflationary policies, for example, simply lead to higher inflation but the same rate of unemployment.
- include diagrams of the Phillips curve adjustment process to support the arguments made.

2. To answer this question effectively you should:
   - explain unemployment and inflation
   - outline the short-run Phillips curve
   - analyse why demand-side policies might increase inflation and reduce unemployment in the short run
   - analyse the possible fall in real wages if prices rise and nominal wages are slow to adjust and explain how this leads to more being employed.
   - analyse how the labour market may return to the NAIRU as nominal wages change in line with inflation.
   - discuss differing views of the adjustment process to long-run equilibrium – how long does it take according to the Keynesian and classical views?
   - include diagrams of the Phillips curve adjustment process to support the arguments made.

Page 70 Short-Run and Long-Run Aggregate Supply

QUICK TEST

1. The quantity of final goods and services supplied at each and every price in an economy over a given time period
2. Real wages show the purchasing power of money wages, i.e. they are adjusted for inflation
3. Real wages are reduced (the purchasing power of the money wages is reduced)
4. Contracts may be fixed for some time; employees may not like the idea of a money wage cut; many employees do not appreciate what is happening to prices
5. Real wages increase and reduce the quantity demanded of labour
6. Keynesians believe the labour market is slow to adjust and return to the long-run equilibrium; the economy can stay below its potential output for some time; classical economists believe the labour market clears more quickly and the economy is generally at or near its potential output
7. Boosting demand would simply lead to inflation and no reduction in unemployment – better to improve aggregate supply
8. The economy can get stuck below its potential output and boosting demand would help restore it to long-run equilibrium more quickly than waiting for money wages to fall
9. Improve the long-run productive potential of the economy, e.g. through training, investment, better technology

PRACTICE QUESTION

1. To answer this question effectively you should:
   - explain the meaning of aggregate demand (AD = C + I + G + X – M)
   - explain how the government can increase aggregate demand, e.g. through lower taxation rates or increased government spending on final goods and services
   - explain that the impact of an increase in demand depends on where the economy is at the time (or at the time when an increase in aggregate demand takes effect), e.g. if the economy is at its potential output, an increase in aggregate demand leads to more inflation but does not reduce unemployment.

In this situation, supply-side policies would be more effective as demand-side polices affect prices more than output. If the economy is below its potential output, an increase in demand may pull up prices, reducing real wages and increasing demand for labour. This can reduce unemployment and also increase prices. The effect of an increase in aggregate demand depends, therefore, on the price elasticity of aggregate supply. In the long run, when aggregate supply is vertical (price inelastic), an increase in demand is simply inflationary. If aggregate supply is not completely price elastic (i.e. in the short run), an increase in demand can reduce unemployment.
- highlight the difference between the Keynesian view (that increasing aggregate demand would be effective) and the classical view (that an increase in demand is inflationary)
- support your answer with diagrams of aggregate demand and short-run and long-run aggregate supply.

Day 5

Page 74 Financial Markets

QUICK TEST

1. The spot rate is the present rate at which currency can be exchanged; a forward rate occurs when the rate at which a currency can be changed into another in the future is fixed
2. An IOU
3. (5% of £50) £2.50
4. Debt is borrowing; equity occurs when funds are raised by selling shares
5. The primary market is where shares and bonds are first sold; the secondary market occurs when existing shares and bonds are bought and sold
6. The yield will fall as the coupon will be a smaller percentage of the price of the bond

PRACTICE QUESTION

1. To answer this question effectively you should:
   - explain that the capital market provides medium to long-term finance to firms
   - explain how firms raise finance through the capital market via equity and debt
   - explain the importance of this for businesses e.g. financing expansion, investment and takeovers
   - outline how the government also raises funds in the capital market, which enables it to run a deficit
   - explain the difference between the primary and secondary capital markets.

Page 78 Banks and Risk

QUICK TEST

1. A snapshot of a bank's financial position at a given moment in time; it shows sources of funds on one side and its use of funds on the other side.
2. The higher the reserve ratio, the less a bank can lend out, which reduces credit creation
3. To make a profit a bank must lend out money; to be liquid a bank must retain some of its deposits to meet demand of customers to withdraw their funds
4. What a bank owns
5. A commercial bank is a high street bank, e.g. Lloyds or Barclays, whose main functions are to accept deposits from savers, lend to households and firms, and provide efficient means of payment.

6. Credit creation is when banks make more loans to individuals and businesses, with the result that the amount of money in circulation increases.
7. Liquidity risk for a bank is when there is a danger that a large number of depositors and investors may withdraw their funds at once, leaving a bank short of funds.
8. Credit risk is the probability that an individual or firm will not be able to pay back a loan.

PRACTICE QUESTION
1. To answer this question effectively you should:
   - outline the functions of a bank
   - explain what is meant by liquidity risk, why it can occur (i.e. if depositors want to withdraw their funds) and how banks might try to reduce it, e.g. by increasing the funds held in reserve
   - explain what is meant by credit risk (i.e. if someone cannot repay their loan) and how banks might try to reduce it, e.g. by assessing the risk of anyone or any organisation it lends to more carefully and taking fewer risks in its lending.

Page 80 Types of Bank and Regulation
QUICK TEST
1. Commercial banks are the high street banks such as Barclays and HSBC; an investment bank specialises in helping companies with their finances, e.g. to raise money, to undertake and finance a takeover and advise on share issues
2. It is responsible for the regulation of around 1700 banks, building societies and other financial institutions
3. When an individual or organisation decides how much risk to take knowing that, if things go wrong, someone else will bear a significant portion of the cost
4. To identify and monitor systemic risks to the UK financial system and take action to remove or limit them. It also supports the economic policy of the government.
5. Systemic risk occurs if there is a danger that problems with one bank could create problems for the whole industry or even the economy
6. Instability can lead to a fall in investment; and greater savings / less spending (which reduces demand)
7. Financial intermediaries involved in the provision of credit across the global financial system, but who are not subject to regulatory oversight.
8. An investment bank specialises in helping companies with their finances, e.g. to raise money, to undertake and finance a takeover, and to advise on share issues.

PRACTICE QUESTIONS
1. To answer this question effectively you should:
   - outline what is meant by the financial system
   - explain the roles of the Bank of England, the Financial Policy Committee (FPC) and the Prudential Regulation Authority (PRA)
   - explain the role of the Financial Conduct Authority (FCA), which works in conjunction with the FPC and PRA but is not part of the Bank
2. To answer this question effectively you should:
   - explain the different elements of the financial system
   - explain the potential risks of the financial system in terms of systemic risk, financial instability and moral hazard
   - explain the ways in which the financial system is regulated, e.g. through the Financial Services Act
   - analyse the overall risk, e.g. the UK financial system probably poses less of a risk to the UK economy than it did, due to greater regulation in recent years. There is now a difference between a

risk to a bank and a risk to the whole banking system. Although, it depends on the extent of the shadow banking system.

Page 84 Money
QUICK TEST
1. Currency; bank deposits; central bank reserves
2. People are are willing to hold it as it is expected to retain its value over time
3. People are willing to accept it as they know they can use it for other transactions
4. People can measure the value of something in money terms
5. The money that consumers have available for transactions; made up of currency and bank deposits
6. Money made up of IOUs from the central bank; currency and central bank reserves
7. Banknotes and coins that are not convertible into another asset such as gold
8. When a bank makes a loan to one of its customers, it credits the customer's account with a higher deposit balance
9. A different type of IOU from the Bank of England, which allows banks to cover the frequent deposit withdrawals and other outflows
10. When the Bank of England was founded in 1694, its first banknotes were convertible into gold – this was known as the 'gold standard'

PRACTICE QUESTION
1. To answer this question effectively you should:
   - outline the functions of money in terms of store of value, medium of exchange and unit of account
   - explain that money may have different forms
   - explain what is meant by base money
   - explain what is meant by broad money.

Day 6
Page 88 Central Banks and Monetary Policy
QUICK TEST
1. The Bank of England is the UK's central bank; it is owned by the government but is responsible independently for monetary policy; it is a banker to government, lender of last resort and regulator of the financial system
2. To set the interest rates it believes are needed to achieve the government's inflation target
3. A scheme aimed at creating incentives for banks and building societies to boost their lending to the UK economy
4. A central bank creates new money electronically to buy financial assets, like government bonds
5. Any two from: saving; borrowing; investment; exchange rates; spending; demand; output; employment
6. The Bank outlines what is likely to happen in the future with interest rates
7. B

PRACTICE QUESTIONS
1. To answer this question effectively you should:
   - outline the role of the Bank of England, e.g. a banker to government, lender of last resort, regulator of financial system
   - outline the role of the MPC in terms of using interest rates to achieve the inflation target
   - show how interest rates may be used to achieve inflation targets, e.g. higher interest rates to reduce demand and put less downward pressure on prices

2. To answer this question effectively you should:
   - outline what is meant by an interest rate and explain its relevance for savers and borrowers
   - state the different economic agents, e.g. households, firms and government
   - analyse the possible effects of lower interest rates on different economic agents, e.g. lower interest rates will affect rewards for saving, cost of borrowing for firms and the government and may affect the exchange rate; they are likely to stimulate demand and can lead to more output and jobs and / or higher prices
   - make a judgement about the impact of lower interest rates, e.g. The effects of lower interest rates may take a couple of years to work through the economy. The effects will vary from agent to agent (e.g. saver vs borrower, exporter vs importer). The effects may depend on how much interest rates fall and for how long they are expected to remain low.

Page 92 Fiscal Policy and Supply-Side Policies
QUICK TEST
1. The difference between government expenditure and income during a year
2. Government income during a year is greater than expenditure
3. An estimate of how large the deficit would be if the economy was operating at a sustainable level of employment
4. A measure of all receipts and current spending, excluding spending on net investment
5. The total amount of money owed at a given moment by a government
6. If there is a budget deficit, this will increase the national debt
7. If the economy is below its 'normal' level, the actual deficit would be higher than the structural deficit – the difference is the cyclical deficit

PRACTICE QUESTIONS
1. To answer this question effectively you should:
   - define tax and explain the different forms of tax e.g. direct and indirect, progressive, proportional and regressive
   - explain taxation as a withdrawal from the circular flow of income
   - explain the effects of a change in direct taxes, e.g. lower income tax may mean more disposable income, leading to more consumption spending and more demand; lower corporation tax means more profits and more investment spending, which will boost demand
   - explain effects of a fall in indirect tax, e.g. lower VAT reduces prices and will stimulate spending
   - state that on its own, a decrease in taxation should boost demand
   - explain the consequences on government objectives such as unemployment, inflation, balance of payments and growth.

2. To answer this question effectively you should:
   - outline the meaning of a government deficit
   - link government deficit to national debt
   - explain why the government may have a deficit at the moment, e.g. relatively high spending and lower taxation revenue
   - explain that a deficit needs financing and this incurs interest costs, which have an opportunity cost; a bigger deficit may require higher interest rates to sell the bonds to finance it
   - Analyse the effect of higher interest rates on the economy and how this may lead to crowding out

   - discuss the view that reduced spending is unnecessary; you may consider the impact of deficit financing vs the impact of reduced spending; you may question the speed and severity of the cuts; you may consider alternative ways of reducing the deficit, e.g. increasing tax revenue and promoting economic growth.

Page 96 Globalisation and Emerging Economies
QUICK TEST
1. A summary measure of average achievement of a number of important dimensions, e.g. health, education and standard of living
2. Economic growth measures increases in income; economic development also considers other issues such as social freedom and the availability of life-sustaining goods and services
3. Any two from: low income per person; low productivity; high levels of natural resources; high dependence on primary products; high levels of external debt; fast population growth; low literacy rates; young growing population; political and economic instability; poor infrastructure; high birth and death rate
4. Any two from: corruption; poor infrastructure; instability of prices of main export products; high levels of external debt
5. Any two from: jobs and income; technology and expertise; investment
6. Any two from: exploitation of local resources; may not take account of external social and environmental costs; fail to share technology, high level jobs or profit
7. Greater integration of economies, industries, societies and cultures around the world
8. New products, greater choice, better quality, export markets
9. May threaten some domestic industries; may change the local way of life and culture
10. Any two from: improved transport and communication links; fewer barriers to trade / fewer protectionist measures; differences in tax systems; containerisation

PRACTICE QUESTION
1. To answer this question effectively you should:
   - state that economic growth focuses on national income, e.g. it is measured by changes in GDP
   - outline that economic development is a broader concept referring to the stage of development a country is at, taking account of social and political development as well as income; you might refer to Todaro
   - explain the factors that influence economic growth and factors that influence economic development
   - explain the limitations of GDP as an indicator of welfare.

Day 7
Page 100 Growth and Development
QUICK TEST
1. Savings and investment are key determinants of economic growth
2. Any two from: bilateral; multilateral; project aid; debt relief; humanitarian
3. Rural agriculture; urban manufacturing
4. Non-governmental organisation
5. Any one from: helps the country develop its own economy / enhance its growth potential; fund infrastructure improvements; improve productivity / develop human capital; helps the country become a market for exports
6. Financial services made available to help entrepreneurs and start-ups

PRACTICE QUESTION

1. To answer this question effectively you should:
   - outline what is meant by a developing country and some of the typical features
   - outline the meaning of free trade and analyse how this might help a country to develop (e.g. access to markets, export revenue boosting domestic demand and encouraging FDI)
   - outline some of the forms of aid and analyse the ways this might help a country develop (e.g. financing infrastructure, developing human capital, funding investment)
   - evaluate these policies, e.g. the potential monopsony power of developed economies may mean lower prices for producers in developing countries; developing economies may struggle to start up in industries where developed economies have first mover advantage; aid may lead to inefficiency; funds may not be targeted or used effectively; effectiveness depends on type of aid and how used; depends on whether it is completely free trade and, if so, the power balance between countries.

Page 104 Trade

QUICK TEST
1. D
2. C

PRACTICE QUESTION
1. To answer this question effectively you should:
   - outline the principle of comparative advantage leading to lower priced items for consumers
   - analyse how trade can lead to consumption outside of the production possibility frontier, providing more goods and services for consumers; consumers can benefit from better quality products that are cheaper than those produced domestically.
   - analyse how trade can lead to growth and internal economies of scale for a business leading to lower prices for consumers.

Page 108 Competing Abroad

QUICK TEST
1. A
2. C

PRACTICE QUESTION
1. To answer this question effectively you should:
   - define free trade
   - define protectionism
   - discuss the reasons for protectionism, e.g. to protect infant industries, retaliate against other countries, protect a way of life or strategic industries; distinguish between political and economic reasons.
   - discuss the problems of protectionism, e.g. subsidising inefficient domestic producers leads to higher prices and worse quality for consumers
   - recognise that the precise impact of protectionism depends on what form is adopted
   - make a judgement, e.g. whether protectionism should be introduced may depend on the reason and duration (e.g. infant industry may lead to efficient domestic production and protectionism may be removed over time); it may depend on what criteria we are judging it by, e.g. is it for political reasons rather than economic? Are we the producers in a protected domestic industry or consumers?

   - consider the long-run likelihood of retaliation by other countries and limitations on the ability of the UK to use protectionism as a member of WTO.

Page 112 The Balance of Payments

QUICK TEST
1. A record of all of a country's financial transactions with the rest of the world over a year
2. The value of money leaving the country on the current account is greater than value of money entering the country
3. To get consumers to switch to domestic products and away from foreign products
4. To reducing total spending in an economy
5. Following a depreciation of the exchange rate, the current account position on the balance of payments may get worse before getting better (as shown by the shape of the curve)
6. The current account position will improve if the price elasticity of demand for exports + the price elasticity of demand for imports is greater than 1
7. To encourage global monetary cooperation, financial stability, more international trade, higher levels of employment, sustainable economic growth and less poverty
8. To ensure the stability of exchange rates and international payments

PRACTICE QUESTION
1. To answer this question effectively you should:
   - define devaluation
   - analyse the possible effects of a devaluation, e.g. its effect on export prices in terms of foreign currency and import prices in domestic currency
   - discuss the importance of the Marshall Lerner condition and the importance of the price elasticity of demand for imports and exports
   - explain how demand for imports and exports is likely to become price elastic over time and how this affects the current account position
   - discuss the J-curve effect
   - compare devaluation with other methods of reducing the deficit, such as expenditure reducing methods; compare the impact on different economic agents, such as consumers, firms and governments
   - make a judgement about the best way to reduce a current account deficit – it may depend on the time period considered (J-curve effect) or income elasticity of demand for imports (if using expenditure reducing methods).

Index

Acknowledgements

The author and publisher are grateful to the copyright holders for permission to use quoted materials and images.

Cover and P1: © Leigh Prather / Shutterstock

P18: SamSingh / Shutterstock; P54: wavebreakmedia / Shutterstock; P104: MAGNIFIER / Shutterstock

All other images are © HarperCollins*Publishers* Ltd

Published by Letts Educational
An imprint of HarperCollins*Publishers*
1 London Bridge Street
London SE1 9GF

ISBN: 9780008179687

First published in 2017

10 9 8 7 6 5 4 3 2 1

British Library Cataloguing in Publication Data.

A CIP record of this book is available from the British Library.

Series Concept and Development: Emily Linnett and Katherine Wilkinson
Commissioning and Series Editor: Katherine Wilkinson
Author: Andrew Gillespie
Project Manager: Rebecca Skinner
Project Editor: Rachel Allegro
Index: Lisa Footitt
Cover Design: Paul Oates
Inside Concept Design: Paul Oates and Ian Wrigley
Text Design, Layout and Artwork: QBS
Production: Natalia Rebow
Printed in Italy by Grafica Veneta SpA

MIX
Paper from
responsible sources

FSC
www.fsc.org

FSC™ C007454